An Introduction To
The Presidential Trend

*A Concise Narrative of One of the
Largest Political Trends*

Tony Fairfax

An Introduction to the Presidential Trend
A Concise Narrative of One of the Largest Political Trends

Book Code: TPT1XA34ED

Cover Photo: Kaufmann Visual Arts

International Standard Book Number: 978-0-9752546-9-1

Library of Congress Control Number: 2015900845

First Edition: June 2015

CONTENTS

An Introduction to the Presidential Trend

LIST OF FIGURES

LIST OF TABLES

An Introduction to the Presidential Trend

ABOUT THE AUTHOR

Mr. Fairfax is a Geodemographic Consultant and President/CEO of the firm CensusChannel LLC. For almost twenty-five years, he has worked as a demographic and mapping consultant with a concentration on census and political data analysis and services. Specializing in redistricting, he has developed several hundred redistricting plans that have covered 22 different states. During the span of his consulting tenure, Mr. Fairfax has provided services and training to numerous private, nonprofit, and public sector groups.

Several highlights of Mr. Fairfax's consulting career have included working as an expert to provide redistricting plans, research, and analysis for several court cases. He has also testified twice as an expert witness in a federal redistricting court case.

Prior to becoming a consultant, Mr. Fairfax worked as an electrical engineer. He worked for a manufacturing division of a Fortune 500 company (Teledyne Inc.) and for a government contracting consulting firm (Engineering & Economics Research Systems).

Mr. Fairfax's prior publications include, *The Presidential Trend* and *A Step-by-Step Guide to Using Census 2000 data*. He has a Bachelor of Science degree in electrical engineering from Virginia Tech. Mr. Fairfax is married to Dr. Colita Nichols Fairfax and has two daughters, Layla and Natalie.

An Introduction to the Presidential Trend

ACKNOWLEDGMENTS

There are too many individuals whom I would like to thank yet simply cannot due to the concise nature of this introductory book. Therefore, to all of my family, friends, and original supporters, I say thank you for everything that you have done. All of you have contributed to my growth as a person in small or large ways, and thus, ultimately, to this book. Once again, I thank you all.

I would be remiss if I did not acknowledge the CBC Institute. When I first discovered the trend, I was reviewing Census Bureau documents for a consulting project at the Institute. I truly believe that I would not have discovered the trend if I had not been working on their project. Thus, my deep gratitude and thanks go to an extremely professional organization with an exceptional board and staff that includes several quality members of congress and superior business professionals.

In addition, I am tremendously thankful to those who gave financial support for my initial publication efforts that led to the development of this book. I am deeply grateful for your heartfelt support and will never forget your contributions.

Finally, I would like to thank an excellent professor and a PhD candidate who work at an outstanding university (Howard University): Dr. Alicia Petersen and soon-to-be PhD, Geoffrey Bell, Jr. Thanks for your help with integrating my book at the college level.

An Introduction to the Presidential Trend

PREFACE

This publication was developed as a condensed version of my book, *The Presidential Trend*. At its core, *The Presidential Trend* describes a major political trend that persisted for almost three decades, in which our country's electorate exhibited the effects of an undetected voting realignment. One of the effects of this realignment was an unusual phenomenon pertaining to the popular vote for president. In addition, the political forces that created this unique trend also created several other unusual voting patterns as well. This book attempts to describe each of these trends as well as their cause and potential future effects.

This book is written to provide the reader with an overview of the original publication. In addition to a condensed explanation of the book's theories, it also includes footnotes directing the reader to the sources of more detailed explanations contained within the original text. Those readers who desire a more comprehensive description of the theory should read the complete version of *The Presidential Trend*.

An Introduction to the Presidential Trend

Chapter 1

A Brief Discussion of the Trend

An Introduction to the Presidential Trend

Introduction

Why did the popular vote for the Democratic nominee for president increase in an unusual straight line for almost 30 years, with the exception of one election? What created this unique voting trend? Did the trend influence the outcome of past presidential elections and could it affect elections yet to come? This book develops a theory that addresses these questions, and offers insights as well as possibly accurate projections for the results of future presidential elections.

This publication is a condensed version of my recently published book, *The Presidential Trend*. The purpose of this book is to consolidate the major components of this consequential phenomenon into a compact version so that the general public can understand and appreciate the trend's significance quickly. Readers who desire a detailed explanation of the analysis and subsequent theory should review the full version of the book.

The Discovery

Many discoveries in the past have occurred by chance. The detection of this unique voting anomaly was no different. I found this unusual pattern when I was conducting a routine review of a collection of data reports for a consulting project.[1] The aforementioned documents were U.S. Census Bureau reports that included the results of several presidential elections. For some reason, I continued to glance back at a particular graph, which depicted votes cast—specifically, the popular vote for president by a major political party between 1972 and 2000. I had seen this graph before, or at least one similar to it, but had never seen the pattern identified on that specific day (Fig. 1-1 contains a copy of the page and graph taken from the 2001 Statistical Abstract of the U.S.).

---

[1] At the time, I was consulting for a project for a newly-formed nonprofit organization called the CBC Institute.

An Introduction to the Presidential Trend

reapportionment following the 1960 census. Members are elected for 2-year terms, all terms covering the same period. The District of Columbia, American Samoa, Guam, and the Virgin Islands each elect one nonvoting Delegate, and Puerto Rico elects a nonvoting Resident Commissioner.

The Senate is composed of 100 members, 2 from each state, who are elected to serve for a term of 6 years. One-third of the Senate is elected every 2 years. Senators were originally chosen by the state legislatures. The 17th Amendment to the Constitution, adopted in 1913, prescribed that Senators be elected by popular vote.

Voter eligibility and participation— The Census Bureau publishes estimates of the population of voting age and the

percent casting votes in each state for Presidential and congressional election years. These voting-age estimates include a number of persons who meet the age requirement but are not eligible to vote, (e.g. aliens and some institutionalized persons). In addition, since 1964, voter participation and voter characteristics data have been collected during November of election years as part of the CPS. These survey data include noncitizens in the voting age population estimates but exclude members of the Armed Forces and the institutional population.

Statistical reliability—For a discussion of statistical collection and estimation, sampling procedures, and measures of statistical reliability applicable to Census Bureau data, see Appendix III.

Figure 7.1
Vote Cast for President by Major Political Party
Millions of dollars

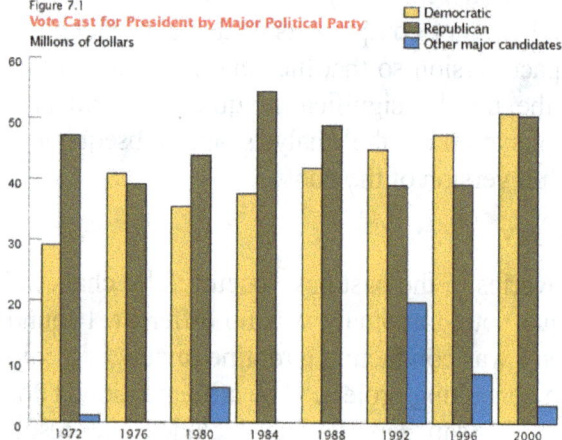

| ☐ Democratic |
| ■ Republican |
| ■ Other major candidates |

¹ 1972—American, John Schmitz; 1980—Independent, John Anderson; 1992—Independent; Ross Perot, 1996 Reform, Ross Perot. 2000—Green, Ralph Nader.

Source: Chart prepared by U.S. Census Bureau. For data, see Tables 378 and 379.

232 Elections

Source: U.S. Census Bureau, Statistical Abstract of the United States: 2001, pg. 232. A typo was removed from the original page

Figure 1-1. Votes Cast for President, US Statistical Abstract, 2001 (1972 to 2000: pg. 232)

4

A Brief Discussion of the Trend

If you do not see the pattern, look at Fig. 1-2 and view a zoomed-in recreation of the same graph with votes cast for the Republican and other major (Independent) candidates removed.

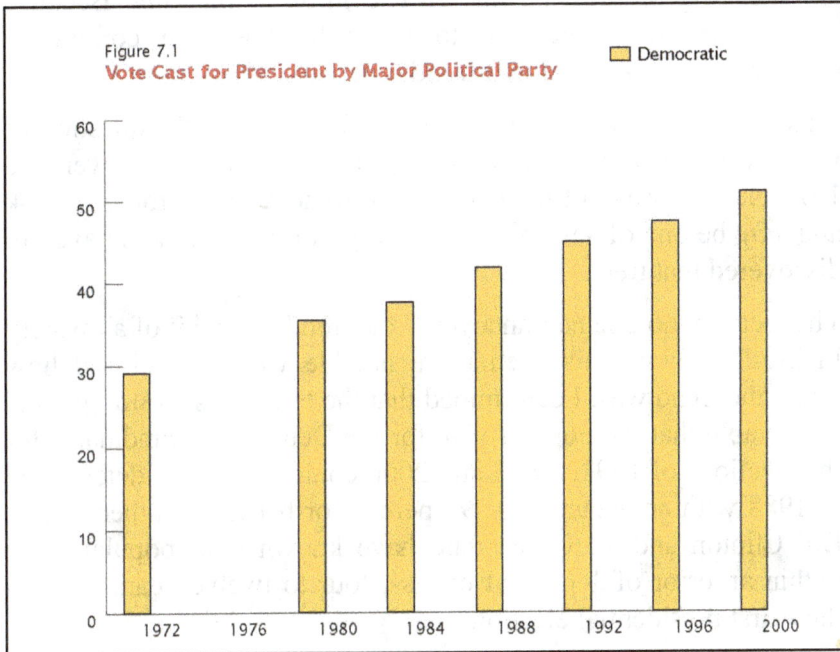

Figure 7.1
Vote Cast for President by Major Political Party

☐ Democratic

Source: U.S. Census Bureau, Statistical Abstract of the United States, 2001, edited

Figure 1-2. Popular Vote for Democratic Presidential Candidates (1972 to 2000)

The popular vote for the Democratic presidential candidate clearly followed a straight line or *linear* trend from 1980 to 2000. Nevertheless, I observed quickly that the trend from 1980 to 2000 seemed to align itself with the election of 1972. At the same time, the trend was not in alignment with the 1976 election.

The fact that the 1976 election was not in alignment with the other elections did not detract from viewing the 1972 to 2000 trend as linear. The rationale for this line of thinking was that, in the world of statistics, there exists a term known as an "outlier."

An outlier is an "observation (or subset of observations) that appears to be inconsistent with the remainder of that set of data."[2] For those who find that statement pure jabberwocky, I am speaking of the well-known *exception to the rule*. Because outliers are the exception to the rule, they are commonly discarded when analyzing a trend.

This did not mean that I would not seek to answer the question of what occurred in 1976 and why it was an outlier.[3] However, the 1976 election was not included in the trend analysis for this book and *may* be one of several reasons why other researchers have not discovered that trend.

The fact that no one had uncovered the trend was a bit of a mystery in itself. I found this even more notable when I analyzed how linear the trend was. I determined that the trend was so straight and predictable that the popular vote for the Democratic candidates for the elections of 1992, 1996, and 2000 could have been determined in 1988 with an accuracy of 99 percent or better.[4] In other words, Bill Clinton and Al Gore could have known their popular vote, within an error of 1 percent or less, four to twelve years prior to their first presidential election run.

Furthermore, from a statistical viewpoint, the 1972 to 2000 linear trend had an astounding R-squared (coefficient of determination) value of 0.997.[5] Without going into too much technical detail, in this instance, R-squared is a number that is calculated to indicate how well the popular vote matched a straight line. A value of "1" would have been a perfectly straight line.

---

[2] Barnett, V., Lewis, T. 1994. *Outliers in Statistical Data.* New York, NY: John Wiley and Sons.

[3] For further details, see *The Presidential Trend*, Chap. 3: "The Exception to the Rule: 1976?"

[4] For further details, see *The Presidential Trend*, Chap. 8: "Projecting the 1992 Election."

[5] For further details, see *The Presidential Trend*, Chap. 7: "Predictable Trend Since 1972."

Nonetheless, once the 1976 election was removed and the Republican and Independent presidential candidates were added back into the graph, an amazing trend for the presidential popular vote was revealed (hence, I titled this voting phenomenon, *the presidential trend*). In order to highlight the linear alignment, I constructed a new graph using a different format (see Fig 1-3).

Figure 1-3 epitomizes the uniqueness of the trend. That is to say, the Democratic popular vote increases in an exceptionally linear fashion, while votes for the Republican and Independent candidates fluctuate.

Democratic, Republican, and Independent Popular Vote (1972 to 2000) w/o 1976

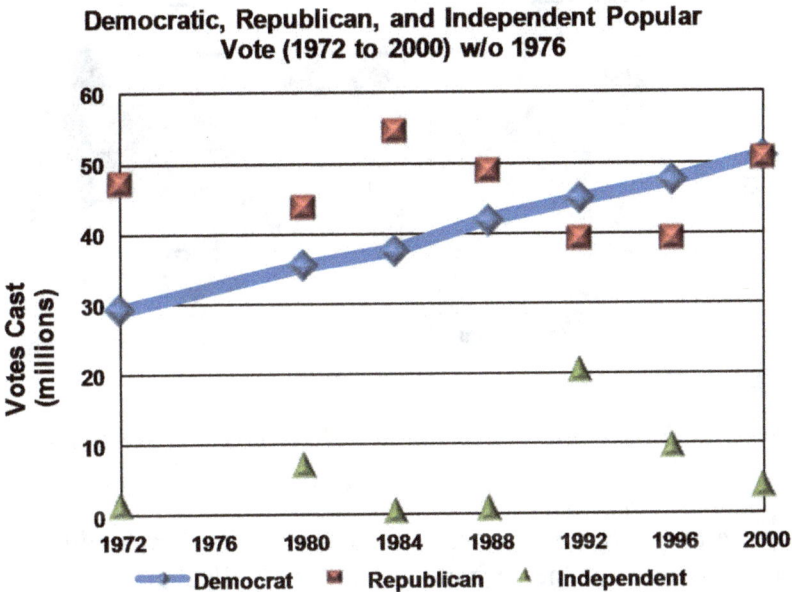

Source: U.S. Census Bureau, Statistical Abstract of the United States, 2001

Figure 1-3. Democratic, Republican, and Independent Popular Vote: (1972 to 2000, w/o 1976)

In some circumstances, a linear trend may not be an oddity. In fact, in many cases, we expect to see a linear trend. For example, most of us have seen linear trends in graphs that depict population growth. However, when I viewed the Republican popular vote over the same period of time, it seemingly showed no visible pattern at all (see Fig. 1-4). I say "seemingly" because I discovered later that there is a second, albeit more obscure, pattern pertaining to the Republican and Independent candidates as well (see Fig. 2-9). In fact, as I ventured on, I discovered not just *one*, but *several*, presidential trends and patterns that have existed and remained in existence in the U.S. electorate (see Chap. 2: "Was there Additional Proof that Validated the Trend?" Chap. 3: "A Baseline Trend", and Chap. 4: "Post Trend Analysis").

Republican Popular Vote in Presidential Elections (1972 to 2000)

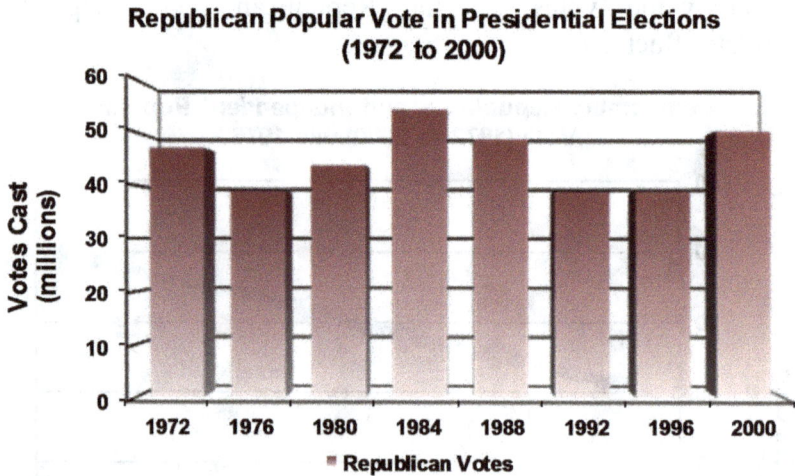

Source: U.S. Census Bureau, Statistical Abstract of the United States, 2001

Figure 1-4. Republican Popular Vote (1972 to 2000)

To reiterate, at first it may have seemed that the Democratic linear trend should be the normal trend, and that the *fluctuating* Republican popular vote was the oddity. This stance was quickly overturned when I realized that each presidential election had different percentages of turnout in the popular vote that *should* have resulted in fluctuations in the votes cast for each major candidate from election to election.

Typically, turnout is defined by how many persons qualified to vote actually do vote. This is defined frequently as a percentage of registered voters or, in some cases, of the population of voting age. To illustrate, look at Fig. 1-5 and review the varying percentages in turnout for the presidential elections from 1972 to 2000. In order for the growth in votes cast to increase in a straight line, there should have been a consistent percentage turnout or at least a steadily increasing pattern.

As Fig. 1-5 indicates, there is no consistent linear pattern in the percentage turnout. The graph shows that, in some elections, there was an increase in the turnout from the previous election; in others, there was a decrease. This makes perfect sense when considering that a variety of different Republican and Democratic candidates, each with differing appeal, should garner different voter turnout.

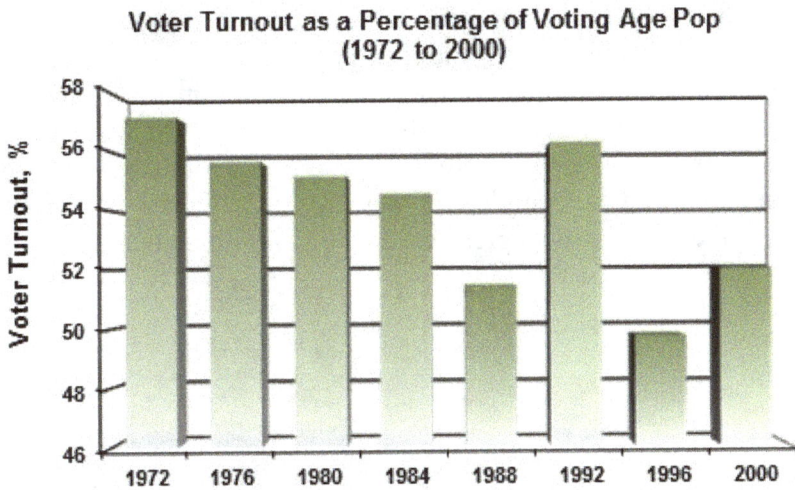

Voter Turnout as a Percentage of Voting Age Pop (1972 to 2000)

Source: U.S. Census Bureau Statistical Abstract of the U.S., 2004 (Table HS-52)

Figure 1-5. Voter Turnout as a Percentage of Voting Age Population (1972 to 2000)

Consider the Republican candidates running in the elections represented in Figure 1-5: Richard Nixon; Ronald Reagan; George H. W. Bush; Bob Dole, and George W. Bush. Now consider the Democratic candidates: George McGovern; Jimmy Carter; Walter Mondale; Michael Dukakis; Bill Clinton, and Al Gore. You can easily see that they encompassed different characteristics and thus should have garnered differing popular votes. In addition to different types of candidates, there are different and distinct issues, different national and global economic conditions, and much more. These potential variations make the linear trend even more astonishing.

Thus, the Republican candidates' popular vote and the overall turnout varied, but the Democratic candidates' popular vote showed a consistently upward and linear trend. After considering the varying conditions from election to election, clearly the oddity was the linear trend of the Democratic candidates and not the varying votes for the Republican candidates (as well as Independent candidates). This discrepancy between the Democratic and Republican popular votes was baffling. How could a linear trend have existed when the voter turnout and other factors varied from election to election? How did the popular vote for millions of voters throughout the country align themselves in a straight and consistent pattern for almost 30 years? These simple questions were extremely thought provoking and the impetus for the development of a completely new political theory that could change the way we view presidential elections dramatically.

Chapter 2

Development of the Theory

An Introduction to the Presidential Trend

Introduction

Within a relatively short period after discovering the trend, several questions needed to be answered. These included:

1. When did the trend begin and end?
2. Why was the trend linear?
3. What caused the trend to be linear?
4. Was there additional proof that validated the trend?
5. What created the realignment in the trend?

With all of these questions outstanding, I set out to research and address them one by one. In the process, I developed a new and possibly groundbreaking political theory.

When Did the Trend Begin and End?

In order to unravel the genesis of the trend, I needed to review the popular vote for elections prior to 1972. This review should assist in addressing whether the trend began in 1972 or earlier.

The first step was to obtain the election results prior to 1972. I turned to two sources: the U.S. Census Bureau and an excellent all-in-one website for past presidential, senatorial, and gubernatorial election results: Dave Leip's *Atlas of US Presidential Elections.*[6]

Using the data obtained, I created several new graphs. The first graph showed the popular vote for the Democratic candidates from 1940 to 2000 (see Fig. 2-1). I felt that 1940 was far enough in the past to find the origin of the trend. In addition, starting in 1940 would far enough in the past to view any additional anomalies that may have been related to the trend.

---

[6] Although the Census Bureau had much of the required information, Leip's website consolidated data into a readily usable format.

As the figure shows, there is no visible indication of a linear trend prior to 1972.[7] For the sake of comparison, a graph of the Republican candidates' popular vote from 1940 to 2000 is shown in Fig. 2-2. Once again, the graph shows no visible consistent linear trend prior to or after 1972.[8]

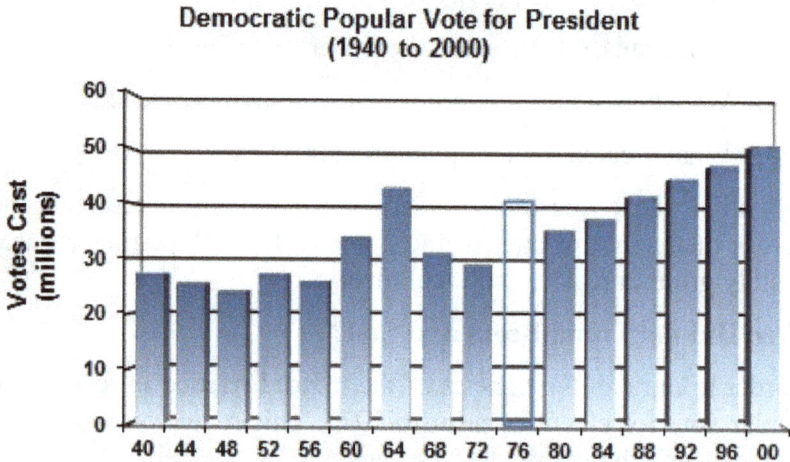

Democratic Popular Vote for President (1940 to 2000)

Sources: U.S. Census Bureau Statistical Abstracts 1942 to 2001 and www.uselectionatlas.org

Figure 2-1. Popular Vote for Democratic Presidential Candidates (1940 to 2000)

There is an additional graph that shows a starker picture of the beginning of the trend (see Fig. 4-5). However, because of its startling *future* implications for the presidential electorate, it will be covered later in last chapter.

---

[7] There is a peculiar voting consistency for 1940, 1944, and 1948 for the Republican and to a lesser extent, the Democratic candidates, which may be researched at a later date.
[8] Some political analysts believe that a major realignment began in 1964 or 1968. However, these theories were directed toward the congress and not the presidency.

The first question had been solved. The trend seemed to have begun in 1972. A second part of the question lingered: when did the trend end?

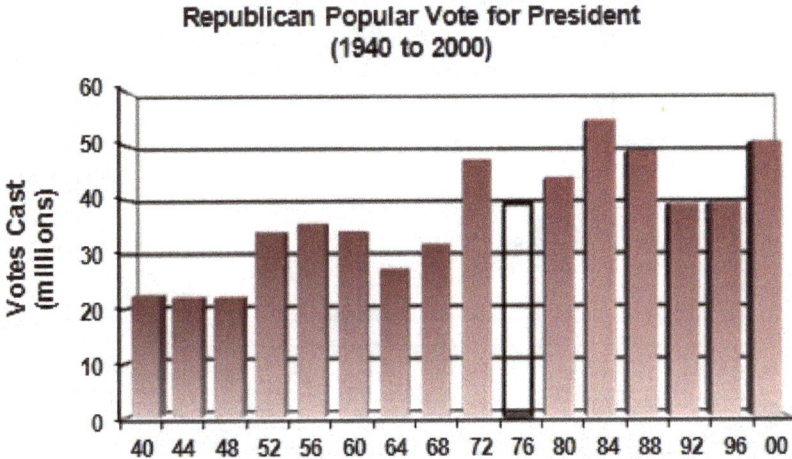

Republican Popular Vote for President
(1940 to 2000)

Sources: U.S. Census Bureau Statistical Abstracts 1942 to 2001 and www.uselectionatlas.org

Figure 2-2. Popular Vote for Republican Presidential Candidates (1940 to 2000)

Of course, the answer to when the trend ended resided with the elections that occurred directly after 2000 (2004, 2008, and 2012). One of the easiest ways to view whether the trend continued was to add the 2004, 2008, and 2012 popular vote to the graph of the trend (see Fig. 2-3). When viewing the trend from 1972 to 2012, the popular vote for the Democratic candidate undeniably began to deviate from the trend line in 2004.

Extending the trend line from 1972 to 2000, the projected popular vote for 2004 should have been close to 54 million. However, the actual popular vote was 59 million. The 2004 projection underestimated the popular vote by over 5 million votes. Likewise, the popular vote for the Democratic candidate for president in 2008 was 12 million votes more than the estimated number using the 1972 to 2000 trend line.[9]

After a significant amount of research, I found that the final explanation for why the trend ended was due to an extraordinary increase in the voting age population, as well as voter registration and turnout.[10] This abnormal step-level increase in voting age population, voter registration, and turnout shifted the trend from its linear path.

Actual vs. Trend Line of the Democratic Popular Vote (1972 to 2012 w/o 1976)

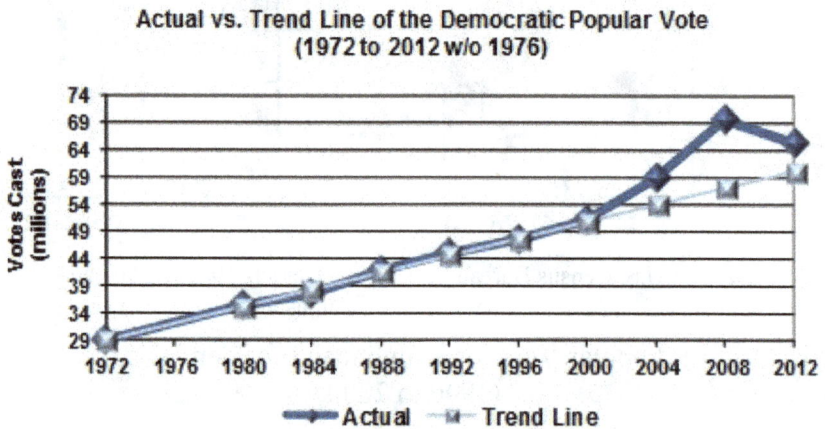

Sources: U.S. Census Bureau Statistical Abstracts 2010 and www.uselectionatlas.org

Figure 2-3. Actual Versus Trend Line of the Democratic Popular Vote (1972 to 2012, w/o 1976)

Why was the Trend Linear?

One of the central questions underlying this political mystery was, *what caused the popular vote for the Democratic candidates to be*

---

[9] For further details, see *The Presidential Trend*, Chap. 14: "The 2004, 2008, and 2012 Elections."

[10] For further details, see *The Presidential Trend*, Chap. 14: "Why a Step-Level Increase in Popular Vote After 2000?"

linear? Of course, this required an initial assumption that a trend such as this would *not* have occurred during normal election cycles. There had to have been some unique circumstance for the popular vote of the Democratic candidates to be extremely linear while the popular vote for the Republican and Independent candidates vary from election to election. In addition, there was one more assumption: something *substantial* must have transpired prior to or during the 1972 election cycle in order for the linear trend to occur. I believed that tens of millions of votes throughout the US would not have aligned themselves for almost 30 years in a linear pattern unless something substantial occurred to the country. As I went through various scenarios of how the popular vote increased in a steadily predictable pattern, I came across a previously created graph that gave me a clue.

The graph in Fig. 2-4 depicts the increase in the voting age population (VAP) from the 1972 to 2000 elections. The voting age population consists of persons above the age of 18 years.[11]

The graph of the VAP was so similar to the graph of the popular vote for the Democratic candidate that I contemplated if there was a connection between the two. After some reflection, I concluded that the connection was that, similar to the VAP, the trend showed a *linear* increase in voting population. To some, this may have seemed like a logical connection to make, but bear with me as I elaborate on why this was important.[12]

With the presidential trend, I expected that the popular vote increased as the voting age population increased. However, the caveat was that the trend seemed to show *only* a consistent increase of new voters and not any fluctuation in votes. This meant that other factors had *not* noticeably influenced the increase in popular

---

[11] Prior to 1972, some state's minimum voting age was older than 21 years or even more.

[12] Registered voters, and specifically the turnout of those voters, is the true measurement of the increase in voters from election to election.

vote for the Democratic candidate—except the increase in the voting population.[13] This included factors such as different election turnout percentages, domestic issues, candidates, or global conditions. Just about any other aspect that you can think of did *not* seem to have an effect on the votes cast for the Democratic candidate.[14] My belief was that if those factors had influenced the votes cast to any appreciable extent, it would have been evidenced by a significant fluctuation in the popular vote.

Voting Age Population in Presidential Elections (1972 to 2000)

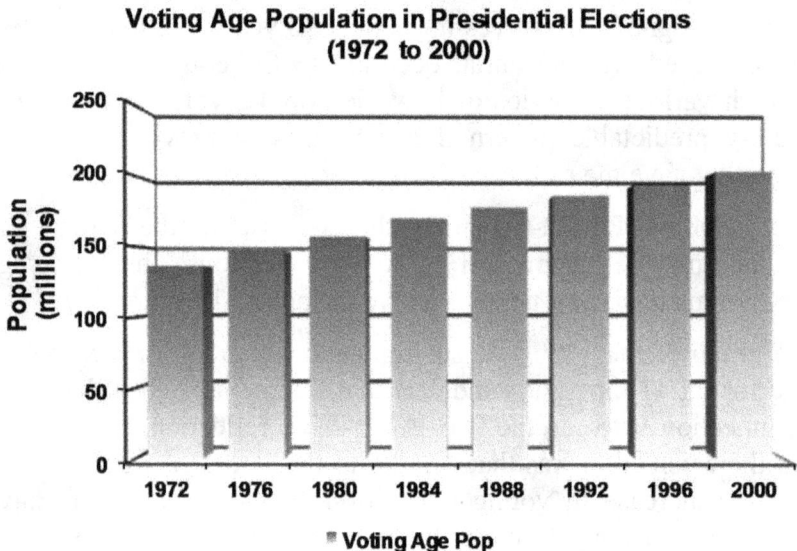

Source: U.S. Census Bureau, Reported Voting Rates in Presidential Election Years by Selected Characteristics, November 1964 to 2004

Figure 2-4. Voting Age Population in Presidential Elections (1972 to 2000)

---

[13] To demonstrate how well the Democratic votes cast related to the overall VAP from 1972 to 2000 (excluding 1976), the ratio of the Democratic popular vote to VAP varied from by only 3.8% (21.4-25.2%), while the Republican popular vote to VAP varied 14.4% (20.2-34.6%).

[14] I later discovered that the total voting age population trend was even less linear than the Democratic popular vote trend.

Development of the Theory

After some contemplation, I determined that the popular vote for the Democratic candidates during this trend period consisted of three major groups of voters:

1) Persons who voted for the Democratic candidate in the previous election;

2) Persons who previously voted for the Republican or Independent Party's candidates in the previous election, and

3) Persons who were first-time voters or did not vote in the previous election.

Here was the beginning of the basis for what I called *the presidential trend theory*. My hypothesis was that the first category, which included voters who voted for the Democratic candidate previously, made up the bulk of the voters in each election. To a lesser extent, the remaining voters came from the second and third categories of voters. These remaining voters included those who *swung over* to vote for the Democratic candidate rather than Republican or Independent candidates, in addition to first-time voters or voters who had not voted in the previous election.

The assumption was that if the second group of voters (the swing voters), was sizable, the trend would have fluctuated significantly from election to election instead. However, if the *net* number of voters in the swing group was *consistent* from election to election, it could be a larger population. This turned out to be the case.[15]

Thus, just as the VAP trend was linear because it consisted essentially of current persons above the age of 18 plus an increase in the group that had just turned 18, the vote for the Democratic candidate was similar. The popular vote for the Democratic candidate was linear because it consisted mostly of voters who voted previously for the Democratic candidate, plus *first-time* voters who also voted for the Democratic candidate. The final and

---

[15] For further details, see *The Presidential Trend*, Chap. 13: "The Swing Voters Who Vote Democratic."

relatively smaller additional group of voters included voters who did not vote in the previous presidential election plus swing voters.

Armed with this new theory, I needed to find a relatively quick way to confirm the hypothesis before moving further into developing a complete theory. The solution to verifying the hypothesis was straightforward. Essentially, if the Democratic popular vote consisted primarily of the previous Democratic voters[16] plus new first-time voters, then the popular vote for a particular election could be *estimated* using these two items. Therefore, I could conduct a simple verification by adding the previous Democratic popular vote plus first-time voters and comparing the sum to the actual results. If the results of this crude analysis were accurate, a more detailed analysis would be warranted.

Data were gathered to test the hypothesis. The previous popular vote data were already available; however, first-time voter information needed to be obtained from exit polls. In this specific case, the 1972 and 1980 elections were *not* used with this technique. For those two elections, the previous elections of 1968 and 1976, respectively, were not appropriate to use.

As previously mentioned, the election of 1976 was an anomaly; an extraordinary number of voters voted for the Democratic candidate. The abundance of Democratic voters would certainly skew the estimate. The election of 1968 had a different problem. First-time voter data for that election were not available. Even if the data were available, this election occurred prior to the completion of the electoral fracturing. Therefore, neither the 1972 nor 1980 election would be appropriate to use for this particular estimation and verification technique.

In order to calculate the popular vote for the 1984 to 2000 elections, the percentages of first-time voters, the partisan portion of those

---

[16] The use of Democratic voters throughout this book refers to voters who vote repeatedly for the Democratic (or Progressive) candidate.

voters, and the number of first-time voters for each party designation were estimated. The accuracy of the calculation was derived using exit poll data and comparing the estimated results to the actual Democratic votes cast.[17] (Chapter 4 of *The Presidential Trend* details the formulas that incorporated exit polls to estimate the popular vote using first-time voters.)

As Table 2-1 indicates, the accuracy of adding the previous popular vote plus the estimated number of first-time voters for the Democratic candidates is no less than 95.4 percent, with an average of 97.5 percent. The table shows that when the same verification check is calculated for the Republican candidates, the accuracy is as low as 69.9 percent, with an average of 83.8 percent.

Table 2-1. Estimate of First-Time Voters and Accuracy of Popular Vote Estimates, 1984 to 2000

	1984	1988	1992	1996	2000
First-Time Democratic Voters (Mil)	2.8	3.0	2.9	4.7	4.9
First-Time Republican Voters (Mil)	4.5	3.3	2.0	2.9	4.1
First-Time Independents Voters (Mil)			1.4	1.0	0.4
Total Democratic Voters Actual (Mil)	37.6	41.8	44.9	47.4	51.0
Total Democratic Voters est. (Mil)	38.3	40.6	44.7	49.6	52.3
Accuracy of Democratic est., %	98.1	97.1	99.5	95.4	97.4
Total Republican Voters Actual (Mil)	54.5	48.9	39.1	39.2	50.5
Total Republican Voters est. (Mil)	48.4	57.7	50.9	42.1	43.3
Accuracy of Republican est., %	88.9	81.9	69.9	92.7	85.8

Sources: *New York Times* exit polls (1980 to 2000) and U.S. Census Bureau Statistical Abstracts 2001

Viewing the results from Table 2-1, the Democratic candidates' popular votes are very close to the actual numbers. However, the estimates for Republican candidates are not as accurate and fluctuate from election to election. The stunning accuracy and

---

[17] Although not displayed, the 1980 popular vote was used in the calculations for the 1984 estimates.

consistency of the estimates for the Democratic popular vote using the previous election plus the first-time voters is another strong piece of evidence validating the initial theory of *the presidential trend*. Nevertheless, further detailed analysis of the makeup of the Progressive electorate reveals a more complex configuration.[18]

Although there was a high rate of accuracy for the estimated number of votes for Democratic candidates, which was astounding, it tended to disagree with conventional political theory. However, once again, there was one vital stipulation: the voters who formed the trend did so in presidential elections. Elections at other levels (congressional, gubernatorial, etc.) may not have displayed aspects of the presidential trend.[19] In other words, these unique voters may have formed a trend *only* when voting in presidential elections. The fact that this trend may only have been visible or even have existed only at the presidential level could be another reason why it had not been discovered thus far. Some analysts lump all voters together despite the type of elections (e.g., a Democratic voter in presidential elections was a Democratic voter in gubernatorial elections or senate elections). In order for this trend to have been viewed and analyzed correctly, only presidential elections should have been analyzed.

I also came to realize that these old and new Democratic voters voted fairly consistently. Simply put, if they did not turn out to vote on a consistent basis, the trend would *not* have been linear. The popular vote for the Democratic candidate would have acted similarly to the popular vote for the Republican candidate. It would have fluctuated with voter turnout, but it did not. Nonetheless, as stated above, a detailed analysis of various exit poll data revealed that the Democratic voters crossed over more than the actual

---

[18] For further details, see *The Presidential Trend*, Chap. 13: "Trend Analysis of Exit Polls by Party Type."

[19] I do believe that this trend, at the presidential level, is the preverbal "canary in the coalmine." In other words, as our electorate becomes increasingly polarized, we could see the trend manifest eventually at lower levels.

results indicated.[20] However, these exit polls were not actual data and may need to be adjusted to the limits of the margin of error.

That said, evidence pointed to the Democratic voters voting consistently from election to election. However, it was important *not* to minimize what it took to ensure that these voters continued to vote in each presidential election. Since the early 1980s, the Democrats have had exceptional voter registration and get-out-the-vote (GOTV) efforts in order to ensure that Democratic voters, specifically the party's base voters, continue to add to the pool of voters and turn out to vote.[21] Without these efforts, the Democratic popular vote *may* have fluctuated. Therefore, the Democratic Party's exceptional voter registration and GOTV efforts may be *one* of the reasons why the trend was sustained for so long.

The answer to the second question was resolved. The trend was linear because the popular vote for the Democratic presidential candidates consisted mostly of voters who voted for the Democratic candidate previously, plus a new group of voters. Each new election cycle continued the pattern of previous Democratic voters and new voters.

Even though the majority of voters were made up of previous Democratic voters and new voters, there was a group of voters who swung back and forth between the Democratic candidates and the Republican or Independent candidates. The hypothesis for these voters was that they constituted either a small number of voters or the net number of voters was relatively consistent from election to election. After exit poll analysis, I determined that these swing

---

[20] For detailed analysis see *The Presidential Trend*, Chap. 13: "The Swing Voters Who Vote Democratic."

[21] Hundreds of progressive civic engagement organizations that tended to focus on underserved communities contributed to increasing and turning out the base. These organizations added to the millions of new registrants and motivated the base to vote.

voters were relatively small and stable[22]. The total number of swing voters, which was relatively smaller than the number of voters who voted for the Democratic candidate previously, was fairly consistent. Hence, after 1972, the popular vote for the Democratic candidate for president consisted largely of: 1) voters who voted for the Democratic candidate previously, plus; 2) first-time voters.

What Caused the Trend To Be Linear?

The final *critical* question in the development of the theory was the most difficult to answer. The previous question addressed the *why* of the linear trend; this question, which seemed to be the same, focused on the *what*. What happened to the electorate that allowed this linear trend to occur?

This question had been nagging me from the very beginning. However, the previous questions had to be answered in order to address this fundamental one. I now had several components of the political puzzle in place, with one large hole in the middle. The pieces of the puzzle already established included:

1) There was no visible indication of the trend prior to 1972 (from 1940 to 1972);

2) A linear trend in the Democratic popular vote began in 1972 and continued to the year 2000 (excluding 1976);

3) The Democratic popular vote from 1972 to 2000 consisted primarily of the Democratic voters who voted for the Democratic candidate previously and Democratic voters voting for the first time, and

4) The Democratic voters tended to vote consistently (possibly due in part to the continued voter engagement efforts).

---

[22] For further details, see *The Presidential Trend*, Chap. 13: "The Swing Voters Who Vote Democratic."

Development of the Theory

I approached this new question by solving a simpler question: Why did the Democratic popular vote only contain essentially Democratic voters after 1972? The answer to this question would undoubtedly lead to the answer desired.

The general answer is simple: something had to occur to the electorate to cause mostly Democratic voters to vote for the Democratic candidate. Furthermore, whatever happened had to be substantial and had to affect the entire national electorate. It was improbable that only a few states affected the national popular vote. Thus, in order to determine what occurred, I had to view the electorate in a unique manner.

Understanding that there had been other times in our electoral history when voting behavior changed, I began reviewing past types of voting trends or analyses. [23] After a short time, I discovered some unique political analysts. One celebrated analyst, Valdimer Orlando Key (V.O. Key), pioneered viewing voter behavior attributes and election results to analyze elections. Another, Louis H. Bean, who was not such an acclaimed analyst (excluding the prediction of one election) [24] used the country's economic conditions to predict election outcomes.

Nonetheless, part of Bean's theory, as well as those of many others, centered on a particular voting trend analogy. This analogy was predicated on the assumption that certain conditions in our country had occurred during which one political party came into power like *tidal waves* coming onto shore. [25] That party would remain in power for a particular period of time. [26] Then, just like tidal waves that roll back out to sea, so would the party's control. Each time this tidal wave occurred, analysts felt that a new political

---

[23] For further details, see *The Presidential Trend*, Chap. 3: "Past Realignments or Trends."

[24] Louis Bean famously predicted the upset of Truman versus Dewey in 1948.

[25] Bean has been credited for developing the concept of *political cycles* or *political tides* (some even compare the cycles to a pendulum swinging).

[26] Usually the realignments last from 30 to 40 years.

realignment also occurred. However, the realignment in the presidential trend was different from the tidal wave analogy. This realignment was not akin to a tidal wave. I determined ultimately that it was more like an *earthquake*. The tidal wave analogy simply did not explain the linear trend phenomenon fully, so I was compelled to expand on this and other similar theories to develop a new one.

At this point, I began this new theory with a central assumption. Because it was clear that the Democratic popular vote was comprised mostly of the previous Democratic popular vote, plus first-time voters, the assumption was that, after 1972, the Democratic popular vote consisted essentially of core Democratic voters. Core voters[27] are those who have a high propensity to vote for the same partisan candidate. Core voters do not need much, if any, persuasion to vote for the Democratic candidate. It is important *not* to confuse persuasion with motivation to turn out. The fact that they were core voters did not mean that they did not require motivation, in some instances, to turn out. The Democratic candidates still required efforts to persuade many of these core voters to vote.

However, once the core voter assumption was made, I quickly realized that if these voters had been the only ones voting for the Democratic candidate, they might as well have been voting in a separate electorate—essentially by themselves. In fact, in order to understand the rationale for the trend, our presidential electorate had to be viewed, not as one, but as *two separate electorates*. Somehow, the presidential electorate had been *fractured* into at least two pieces. A later discovery showed that the electorate did not fracture completely. In reality, a portion of the electorate remained connected, because of a relatively minor group of voters who swung back and forth from electorate to electorate. In addition, it is important to note that the electorate did not actual fracture. It

---

[27] Cox, Gary W. 2010. *Swing voters, core voters and distributive politics, Political Representation*, New York, NY, Cambridge University Press

was not physical entity. Yet, in order to understand what had occurred, this unique theoretical model needed to be simplified and viewed as if the electorate at the presidential level had broken apart completely. [28] What truly occurred to the electorate will be discussed later in this section (see What Created the Realignment in the Trend?).

Consequently, the first portion of the fractured electorate had already been established. It contained mostly core Democratic voters. This portion of primarily Democratic voters explained the existence of the linear trend. This new theoretical electorate that yielded the linear trend in the popular vote contained only voters who tend to vote for the Democratic candidate, plus a consistent number of new Democratic voters.

Initially, this portion in my previous book was called the "Democratic Electorate" since it contained fundamentally Democratic voters. However, it was changed to the "Progressive electorate" to reflect the general political ideological makeup of the voters (see Fig. 2-5). The second portion, which was initially titled, the "Non-Democratic Electorate" because it essentially contained everyone else but Democratic voters, was now titled the "Conservative Electorate."

This second electorate contained voters who voted primarily for the Republican and Independent candidates as well as a sizable number of voters who sometimes did not vote. In addition, the Independent voters included in this electorate represented voters who actually voted for Independent candidates. Many voters have self-identified themselves as Independents but have not voted as such. Lastly, it was recognized that a portion of Independent voters were actually progressive voters (e.g. Green Party). However, they consisted of a relatively small amount of the total popular vote. Thus, in this analysis they remained

---

[28] For further details, see *The Presidential Trend*, Chap. 13: "The Swing Voters Who Vote Democratic."

integrated into the Conservative electorate. The common theme however, was that these voters continued to vote for the "non-democratic" candidate when it came to voting for the office of presidency.

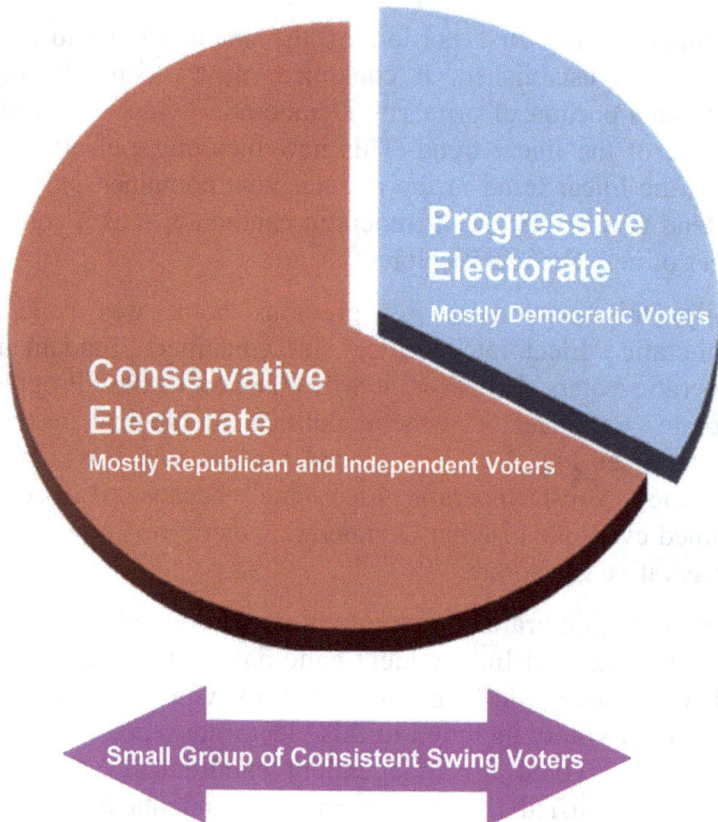

Figure 2-5. Graphical Representation of the Fractured Electorate Post-1972

Therefore, the preliminary question, "why did the Democratic candidates' popular vote contain only or mostly core voters after 1972" was answered. Our voting electorate at the presidential level had been fractured into two pieces. One piece contained largely those who voted for the Democratic candidate, while the other contained essentially voters who voted for the Republican candidate, in addition to those who voted for Independent candidates. [29]

Thus, the answer to the primary question, "what caused the trend to be linear?" was also finally answered. The trend was linear because the electorate fractured into two parts, with one consisting chiefly of Democratic voters. In addition, another critical element of the presidential trend theory had been established. The electorate at the presidential level should be viewed primarily in terms of Democrat and non-Democrat, rather than the usual Democrat and Republican. With the central components of the theory established, I sought additional evidence to validate that the electorate had been fractured.

Was there Additional Proof that Validated the Trend?

Proof of the linear trend was undeniable. There was no doubt that a linear trend existed for the Democratic candidates' popular vote from 1972 to 2000 (excluding 1976). It was measured using standard statistical techniques (revealing an r-squared value of .997). However, given the dramatic nature of this brand-new theory, additional proof was needed that the electorate had been fractured.

To reiterate, the theory was that the electorate fractured into two parts: the first included essentially, only Democratic voters while

---

[29] Expanding this line of thinking, the trend could be viewed in a pure sense as both a minimum (floor or base) and a maximum (ceiling) of votes cast for the Democratic candidate for president. Viewing this trend as a *minimum*, the Democratic candidate's voters were mostly core voters who voted for the Democratic candidate most of the time and other election year's votes should not go below this minimum. Viewing the fractured electorate as a *maximum* depends on the circumstance whereby the Democratic candidate was unable to pull over a significant number of the voters in the Conservative electorate and thus constituted a maximum of votes obtained by the Democratic candidates.

the other, the Conservative or Non-Democratic side, included Republican and Independent voters (see Fig. 2-5). There was recognition that some progressive voters (e.g. Green Party) existed in the Conservative side. However, they represented a small amount. There was also an assumption that there still existed a small portion of each electorate that crossed over, nevertheless this was not a major number either. Thus, if the electorate had truly been fractured for the most part, resulting in a linear trend, what other evidence than that trend might be visible due to this fracturing? Could there have been some other trend or trends created due to the fracturing? I set out to consider each electorate separately and attempted to discover additional proof that validated my hypothesis of a fractured electorate.

To verify the Progressive side, I needed proof to show that this portion of the electorate contained only one set of voters. These were voters who essentially voted only for the Democratic candidates. If the electorate was fractured, the Democratic candidates were isolated from those who voted for the Republican or other Independent candidates. Because this portion of the electorate consisted only of those who voted for Democratic candidates, there should have been some evidence that the votes cast for the Democratic candidates were *not* affected by the votes for the Republican or Independent candidates, or even both.

This assumption relied on the fact that in normal elections, one candidate usually pulls votes away from the other. However, if voters were voting only for a *single* candidate, that should not be the case. This meant that there should be no decrease in the Democratic candidates' votes with an increase in votes for Republican or Independent Party candidates or both.

Therefore, the votes for the Democratic candidates needed to be compared with those for the Republicans and then with those for the Independent candidates. If these two were plotted on a line graph, there should have been a visible dip in the graph of one candidate's votes with an increase in the other. If this increase and decrease relationship was visible, it would be an indication that votes were being *pulled* from one candidate to another. If there was no appreciable reduction, that would tend to validate that the two were isolated from each other.

The Democratic and Republican candidate graphs are presented in Fig. 2-6. Reviewing this graph, the chart reveals that there is no noticeable evidence that one candidate is pulling votes away from the other.

**Democratic and Republican Popular Vote
(1972 to 2000) w/o 1976**

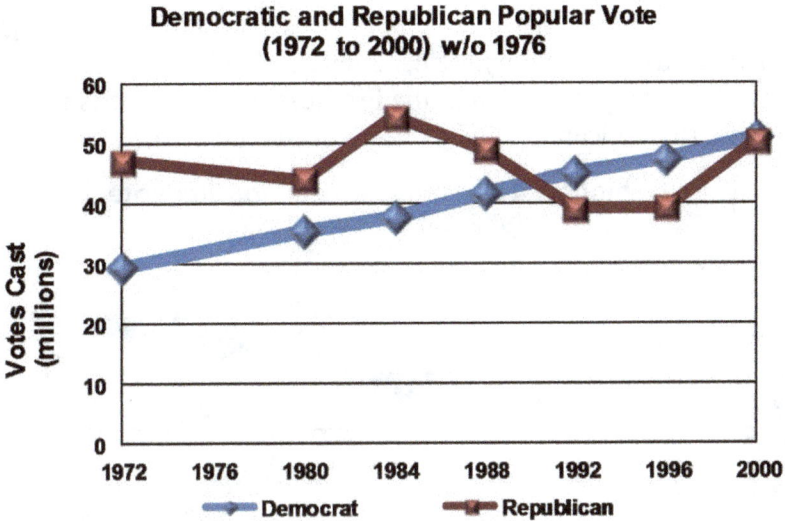

Sources: U.S. Census Bureau Statistical Abstracts 1972 to 2001 and
www.uselectionatlas.org

Figure 2-6. Democratic and Republican Popular Vote
(1972 to 2000, w/o 1976)

Under normal circumstances, votes cast for the Republican candidates should have had some effect on the Democratic candidates' votes or vice versa. Clearly, the graph showed none. Excited with the results of the first test, I plotted the Democratic and Independent party's candidates' votes to determine if they had any effect on one another (see Fig 2-7). There was one quick notation on the votes plotted for the Independent candidates. This analysis and others in this book relied on lumping all of the Independent candidates into one category.[30]

Again, because the Progressive electorate contained mostly votes for the Democratic candidate, there should not be any significant effect of the votes cast for the Independent candidates on the Democratic candidates or vice versa. As Fig. 2-7 shows, once again there is no noticeable effect. These two graphs tend to validate the theory that the Democratic side contains only voters who voted for the Democratic candidates. Plainly, these two charts show additional evidence that the Progressive electorate is isolated from the Republican and Independent candidate's voters.

Democratic and Independent Popular Vote (1972 to 2000) w/o 1976

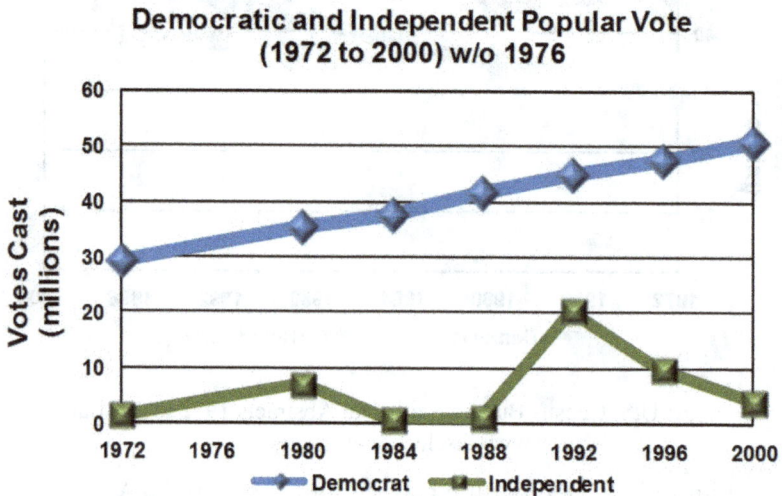

Sources: U.S. Census Bureau Statistical Abstracts 1942 to 2001 and www.uselectionatlas.org

Figure 2-7. Democratic and Independent Popular Vote (1972 to 2000, w/o 1976)

---

[30] There is recognition that some Independent voters may actually oppose the Republican and Independent candidates. However, they represent a small number of the total voters and do not affect the overall analysis.

Development of the Theory

Armed with this proof of the isolation of the Progressive electorate, I considered, what would the other side of the fractured electorate show? In the theoretical other electorate, the Conservative side, there were essentially two types of voters: those who voted for the Republican candidates and those who voted for Independent candidates.

The method previously used to validate that the Progressive electorate contained *one* type of voter showed that the Democratic candidates' votes were not affected by votes for the Republican or Independent candidates. For the Conservative electorate, a different method had to be devised that showed evidence that *two* types of candidates were contained in the second electorate. I looked for a voting pattern that reflected the existence of only two categories of candidates—in other words, almost the opposite of the Progressive electorate. The pattern contained should reflect two types of candidates or parties directly *pulling* voters away from the other.

The method developed to verify that only two categories of voters were contained in the Conservative electorate was to detect a symmetrical or inverse relationship or what I termed the "mirror effect."

To illustrate the *ideal* mirror effect, I present the graph in Fig. 2-8, which depicts a simple two-party race. The graph shows a unique pattern clearly, which creates a *mirroring* or symmetrical pattern in the two different party's votes.

The reason why the mirror image exists in the graph is due to the two candidates vying for the same voters. The two combined make up the total votes counted. In the example, if 60 voters turned out to vote, and one party received 47 votes, then the other party must have received 13 votes. If one party received 45 votes, then the other party must have received only 15 votes. Essentially, one party receives a certain amount of votes, while the other receives the remaining amount. This example of ideal mirroring assumes 60 voters total for each election and, more importantly, every voter votes. If the turnout in total votes fluctuates, the *ideal* mirror pattern is not produced. This of course is what occurs under realistic conditions. Therefore, it is extremely improbable to have an exact mirror image under true electoral conditions. In addition, if a third party was incorporated on to the graph, the mirror effect would diminish and could disappear altogether. Consequently, if the actual results plotted on a graph show a propensity for one party to mirror the other, it should be an excellent indicator of the presence of only two parties.

Thus, if I could find a pattern similar to the one shown in Fig. 2-8, it would provide evidence that *only* two types of candidates existed in the Conservative electorate and additional evidence of the fracturing of the electorate.

Example of Mirroring of Votes Cast for Two-Party Races

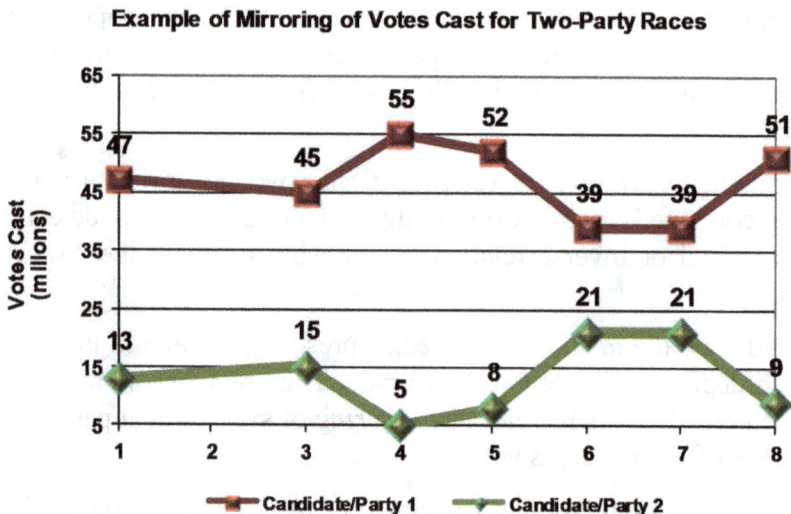

Sources: U.S. Census Bureau Statistical Abstracts 1942 to 2001 and
www.uselectionatlas.org

Figure 2-8. Example of Mirroring Votes Cast in Two-Party Races

As a result, I plotted the votes cast for the Republican and the combined votes of all Independent Party candidates on a graph. As before, I was astonished when I saw the graph in Fig. 2-9. It showed a distinct mirroring of Republican and Independent candidates' votes.

**Republican and Independent Popular Vote
(1972 to 2000 w/o 1976)**

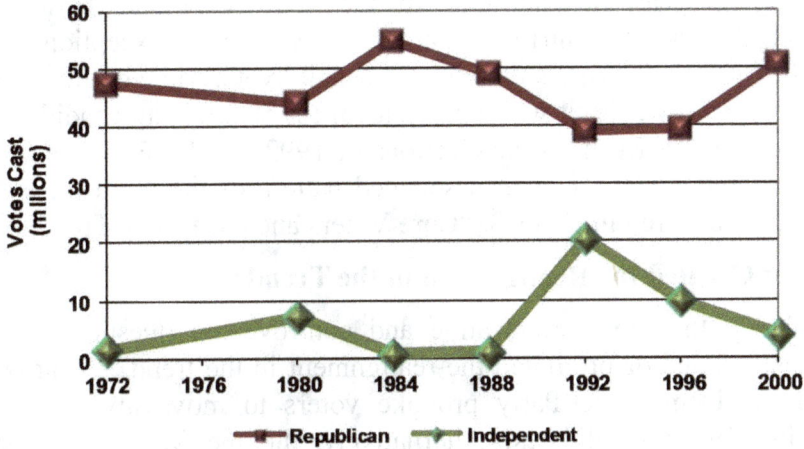

Sources: U.S. Census Bureau Statistical Abstracts 1942 to 2001 and
www.uselectionatlas.org

Figure 2-9. Republican and Independent Popular Vote
(1972 to 2000, w/o 1976)

Nevertheless, as you can see, the result is not two perfectly symmetrical images, although a mirroring of each line graph is clearly visible. First, according to the figure, the total number of votes cast for Republican and Independent candidates fluctuates from election to election. This is unlike the ideal conditions that are depicted in Fig. 2-8, which includes the same total of votes for each election. Second, there are actually three major options for voters in the Conservative Electorate: 1) vote for the Republican candidate; 2) vote for one of the Independent Party candidates, or 3) not vote at all. The third option could be the reason why the image of the votes for the Republican candidate and the combined votes for the Independent Party candidates do not mirror each other perfectly. Most likely, there are elections in which voters either turned out at a higher than usual rate or simply did not vote. These situations are undoubtedly reflected in the graph.

The point on the graph that did *not* produce a mirror effect to the same degree as the other elections occurred in 1992. It seemed that during that year, the leading Independent Party candidate, H. Ross Perot, distorted the mirroring pattern by performing exceptionally well. Essentially, voters that did not usually vote, came out to vote for Perot. However, it was the results of the Republican candidate, George H. W. Bush, in the elections of 1992 and 1996, which led me to contemplate another associated pattern of the trend theory, which is covered in Chap. 3, "Core Voters and a Baseline Trend."

What Created the Realignment in the Trend?

Probably the most provocative and controversial question was, "what created or promoted the realignment in the trend?" That is, did the Democratic Party provoke voters to move away from voting for its candidates? Alternatively, did the Republicans or Independent candidates offer something that shifted voters toward their candidates? These questions sound similar, yet there are subtle differences between the two.

My hypothesis was that voters moved away from the Democratic presidential candidates or party. The key to this hypothesis was the Independent voters. The focal point of the fracturing in voters seemed to be the Democratic candidates. It was as if a portion of the country's voters were determined to vote for anyone but the Democratic candidates. Although there was evidence that there was some crossover from the Progressive electorate to the Conservative electorate, the number seemed relatively small.

Thus, the Independent voters, and possibly some Republican voters, made a conscious decision to shift away from the Democratic candidates and party. In order for this to have occurred, those voters must have disagreed with Democratic policies or initiatives to such a degree that this portion of the electorate would not vote for the Democratic candidate for the next 30 years or more (excluding 1976).

With this hypothesis established, research could begin on what occurred to create this unique voting realignment. Because the trend began in 1972, the natural starting point was a review of that election. In that election, the Democratic candidate was Senator George McGovern and the Republican was President Richard Nixon, who was seeking his second term. Nixon won that election in what was considered a landslide. He won 49 states to McGovern's one and the District of Columbia. McGovern's platform included a fundamental issue: ending the Vietnam War.[31] On the other hand, Nixon also promised that peace in Vietnam was approaching by continuing to implement his policies. Because both sides were promising that they would end the war, it could not have been the *major* occurrence that fractured the electorate. Vietnam may have played some role (most likely in the years to come), but not the dominant one that fractured the electorate.

McGovern was also labeled by Nixon as "too liberal for the country." Nixon reinforced a statement by Senator Thomas Eagleton that McGovern is for "Amnesty, Abortion and Acid."[32] Under normal circumstances, that statement may not have been unusual. However, Eagleton just happened to have been selected as McGovern's vice presidential candidate. Later, McGovern fired Eagleton and selected Sargent Shriver as his running mate. Nonetheless, this liberal label attached to McGovern was not enough to fracture the voting electorate and establish a trend for the next three decades. Once again, the liberal aspect of the Democratic candidate played a role in the fracturing, just not the primary one.

After reviewing the events of the 1972 election, I found no evidence sufficiently substantial to fracture the electorate. As I continued to research, I recalled that the presidential election of 1968 was considered by some political analysts to be a "realigning election."[33] The election ended the dominance of the Democratic

---

[31] McGovern also promised to institute programs that would guarantee income to the nation's poor.

[32] *Time*. August, 1972. "The Eagleton Affair."

[33] The sheer existence of the trend confirms the reality of some type of realignment.

Party that began with Franklin Roosevelt in 1932.[34] In fact, Kevin Phillips, an aide to Richard Nixon, wrote that after the 1968 election, *realignment* occurred whereby the southern region of the country would ultimately become Republican. [35] Therefore, I contemplated, *what if the trend began in 1972, but the fracturing actually occurred in 1968?*

What came to mind about the 1968 election was that it exemplified the decade of the sixties. In fact, some call the sixties the "turbulent sixties."[36] Throughout the sixties, there was a growing divide in the country due to several polarizing issues, such as the increase in recreational drug use, a new sexual revolution, the women's liberation movement, the prolonged war in Vietnam, and of course, civil rights. The unique aspect of most of these major issues in the sixties was that they were all dividing the country's population into *liberal* (or progressive) and *conservative* groups. Consequently, this growing division of our society was literally segmenting the population and at the same time dividing our electorate in two. With the convolution of these divergent issues, our country and electorate were being stretched to the breaking point throughout the sixties. It was simply a matter of time before one of the issues became a catalyst for a major electoral realignment.

To continue, in 1968, both Dr. Martin Luther King, Jr. and Robert "Bobby" Kennedy were assassinated, race riots proliferated throughout the country, violence occurred at the 1968 Democratic convention, and there were widespread protests against the Vietnam War. Politically, thanks to these events, and the fact that President Lyndon Johnson decided not to seek an additional term, the Democratic Party and much of its voting electorate were left in disarray.

---

[34] Franklin Roosevelt's New Deal caused millions of Republican voters to become Democratic.

[35] Rae, N.C. 1994. *Southern Democrat.* New York, NY: Oxford University Press.

[36] For further details, see *The Presidential Trend*, Chap. 2: "The Turbulent 60s."

Because the Democratic Party had no clear-cut succession of leadership, some scholars believe that the 1968 convention, which was designed to choose a presidential candidate and leader, was divided into several factions:[37]

1) Big-city party bosses, led by Mayor Richard Daily of Chicago, Illinois. This faction supported Senator Hubert Humphrey;

2) Followers of Senator Eugene McCarthy, who were comprised mostly of activists against the Vietnam War;

3) Catholics, African Americans, and other racial and ethnic minorities. These individuals were rallying behind Senator Robert Kennedy, and

4) White Southern Democrats or (former) Dixiecrats. Some members supported Hubert Humphrey; however, most of them would end up supporting Alabama's Governor George Wallace.

The particular faction that stood out to me was the fourth group, which consisted mostly of white Southern Democrats. As some may recall, Alabama's George Wallace *split*[38] from the Democratic Party and led the charge to join and expand the American Independent Party. In 1968, George Wallace received over 9.9 million votes or 13.5% of the popular vote. This was the largest total third-party vote since 1924.[39]

As a quick refresher, several years before (in 1962), Wallace was elected governor of Alabama on a pro-segregation, pro-states' rights platform. He won a landslide victory. He gave his most infamous speech at his *inauguration*, which included the statement:

---

[37] Converse, P.E., Miller, W.E., Rusk, J.G. & Wolfe, A.C. 1969. Continuity and change in American politics: Parties and issues in the 1968 election. Wikipedia, United States Presidential Election, 1968.

[38] I later determined that the term "split-off" is a perfect description of what occurred.

[39] In 1924, Republican Robert M. La Follette received 4,831,706 votes for 16.6% of the popular vote in the Progressive Party.

"In the name of the greatest people that have ever trod this earth, I draw the line in the dust and toss the gauntlet before the feet of tyranny, and I say segregation now, segregation tomorrow, segregation forever."

In 1963, Wallace made news again by standing in front of the auditorium at the University of Alabama in order to stop two black students, Vivian Malone and James Hood, from enrolling.[40] Using his public image, Wallace ran, albeit unsuccessfully, for the Democratic nomination for president in 1964. In the 1968 election, his prior words and track record still resonated with many voters. Wallace, this time, ran under the American Independent Party that opposed the 1964 Civil Rights Act vehemently. It was not that they simply opposed the 1964 Civil Rights Act; they opposed federal efforts to end desegregation, including the 1965 Voting Rights Act and the 1968 Civil Rights Act (also known as the Fair Housing Act). The Civil Rights Act of 1964 prohibited discrimination in public facilities and certain employment practices; the Voting Rights Act of 1965 prohibited discriminatory practices in voting, and the Fair Housing Act of 1968 outlawed discrimination in the sale or rental of housing.

The statement that President Johnson purportedly made to his press secretary (Bill Moyers) after signing the Civil Rights Act was prophetic: "I think we have just delivered the South to the Republican Party for a long time to come."[41] Johnson felt instinctively that a portion of the country, specifically the South, was not ready for the change that was about to occur due to the civil rights legislation enacted. He knew that, although polls indicated a majority of the country tended to favor the Civil Rights Act, there was a segment of the population that opposed it

---

[40] Also in 1963, Dr. Martin Luther King, Jr., "called out" Gov. Wallace in his famous 'I have a dream' speech." However, he did not specifically use his name. http://www.archives.gov/press/exhibits/dream-speech.pdf, page 5.

[41] Clymer, A. Divisive words: News analysis; GOP'S 40 years of juggling on race. *New York Times*. 2002.

adamantly. For example, 62% of those surveyed in the Harris Poll of April 1964 stated they favored such a law. Similar findings were made regarding the Voting Rights Act. A Gallup poll taken in the spring of 1965 showed that 75% favored federal voting rights legislation. [42] Sixty-two and Seventy-five percent are very favorable results. However, the real question is, how adamant were those who did not support the legislation? If these voters were sufficiently unyielding, these laws just might have been the catalyst for them to break away from a particular party.

As a case in point, a 1965 Gallup poll showed that 42% of the population indicated that the government was moving too fast in implementing voting rights legislation.[43] Although the implications of this poll are fascinating, the polling preceding the 1968 Fair Housing Act was much more revealing. In 1967, a Gallup poll declared that between 1963 and 1965, 69 to 71% of *Whites* said they might move or would move if a great number of *Negroes* (the term used at that time) moved into the neighborhood.[44] Shortly after the data were collected for that poll, the 1968 Fair Housing Act was passed.

The purpose of the last few pages was not to provide a mini-lesson in civil rights or the racial tensions of the sixties. The purpose was to set the tone for the conditions of that time. It was becoming clear that, after two prior seminal civil rights acts, the 1968 Fair Housing Act was to become the well-known *last straw* for a certain segment of the population. Furthermore, as a direct beneficiary, George Wallace garnered the support of millions of voters who were disgruntled with the country's political climate, specifically regarding civil rights policies (in addition to the other polarizing issues of that time). More importantly, regardless of the fact that several Republican members of congress voted for the

---

[42] Isserman, M. & Kazin, M. *America Divided*, pg. 142.
[43] Gallup, G. & Gallup, Jr., A. 2000. *The Gallup Poll 1999*, pg. 237.
[44] Bonastia, C. *Knocking on the Door: The Federal Government's Attempt to Desegregate*. Princeton, NJ: Princeton University Press, 2006, pg. 88.

Civil Rights Acts, these policies were perceived by the general population as being championed by the Democratic president at that time and ultimately, by the party.

Hence, the Wallace voters were the *key* to the presidential trend. Once I realized that Wallace obtained a substantial number of votes, mostly from former Democrats disillusioned with the path that the country was taking, it became apparent that civil rights legislation was most likely the primary catalyst that fractured the electorate. Although there were additional reasons for the Wallace voters to break off, states' rights, race or civil rights was in the forefront for the 1968 election.[45]

To attempt to corroborate this claim, I added the 1968 election to the previous trend graph. The popular vote for the 1968 election, along with the popular vote for the presidential elections from 1972 through 2000 can now be compared (see Fig. 2-10).

In reviewing the graph, it became obvious that the 1968 Democratic popular vote was approximately the same as in the 1972 election. Returning to the original theory, the hypothesis was that the fracturing of our electorate occurred in 1968. The second part of the hypothesis was now apparent. The fracturing occurred because many of the Wallace voters *split off* and decided not to vote for the Democratic presidential candidate. When this fracturing occurred, essentially only the staunch core of Democratic voters continued to vote for the Democratic candidate.

Nonetheless, Senator Hubert Humphrey, the Democratic candidate in 1968, garnered more votes than did Senator George McGovern in 1972. This led me to conclude that the fracturing (or shifting of voters) occurred, but was not fully complete in 1968. In 1968, a small number of Humphrey's voters did *not* break off and instead continued to vote for the Democratic candidate. However, in the election of 1972, these voters ultimately did break off, leaving an

---

[45] Gould, L. 1993. *1968: The Election that Changed America.* Chicago, IL: Ivan R. Dee, Inc.

even smaller core of Democratic voters. In 1972, these voters became the initial starting point for the Progressive electorate and the beginning of the *presidential trend.*

Democratic Popular Vote in Presidential Elections (1968 to 2000)

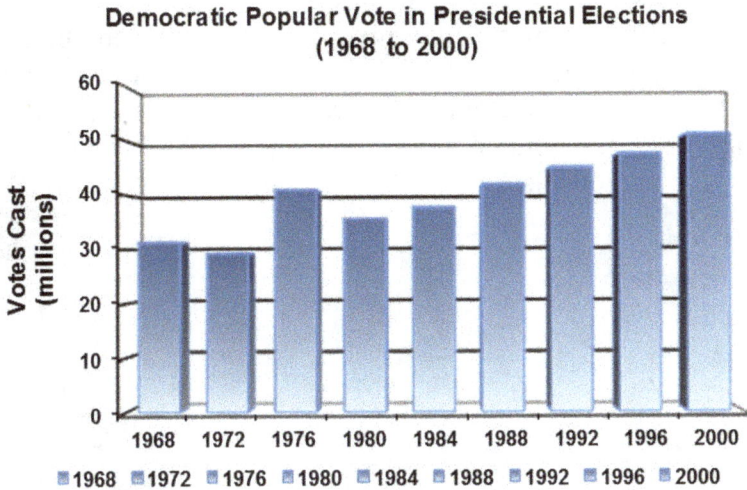

Sources: U.S. Census Bureau Statistical Abstracts 1942 to 2001 and www.uselectionatlas.org

Figure 2-10. 1968 to 2000 Democratic Popular Vote

At this moment, it is difficult not to think of our country's conditions approximately one hundred years prior to this time in the sixties. One hundred years prior, our country was going through a different type of fracturing. During that time, several states succeeded from the union. The catalyst for that particular fracturing also centered on a civil right—a very fundamental one— the right to be free and the end of slavery. In this first fracturing, the country did *not* have theoretical separate electorates; it literally had two distinct electorates.

Nevertheless, in the 1960s, our country had evolved and consequently did not go through a succession like the one that occurred one hundred years earlier. Still, a different type of succession occurred, a succession of the vote that was akin to a second fracturing of the electorate.

There is one final note on the fracturing. It was also determined that civil rights as well as the other divisive issues of the sixties were supplemented by and supplanted with new issues over the next 30 years. The new issues, deemed "wedge" issues, of the seventies, eighties, nineties, and two thousands included abortion, gay rights, gun control, immigration reform, and more.[46] These issues kept the two electorates separated for decades. In fact, it *appears* that they remain separated (see Chap. 4, "2016 and Future Implications").

---

[46] Hillygus D. & Shields T. 2008. *The Persuadable Voter: Wedge Issues in Presidential Campaigns*. Princeton, New Jersey: Princeton University Press.

Chapter 3

Core Voters and a Baseline Trend

An Introduction to the Presidential Trend

Introduction

Many theories spawn additional and supplemental ones. The presidential trend is no different. By observing that the trend centers on voters who vote repeatedly for the Democratic candidate, we see that these voters, in essence, constitute the *core* or *base* voters. The presidential trend could *not* occur without the existence of a core group of voters. Tracking the growth of these core voters from election to election forms what could be called a "baseline trend." After 1972, the popular vote for the Democratic candidate consists mostly of its core voters and is principally the Democratic baseline trend.[47] However, what about a Republican or Independent candidate's baseline? Do they exist?

A Baseline Trend

Figure 2-9, which depicts the Republican and Independent candidates, reveals another peculiarity besides the mirror effect. The graphs of Republican and Independent votes are almost mirror images. The election on the graph that does *not* follow the mirror pattern completely was that in 1992. When considering the additional voters who *turned out* to vote for Ross Perot in 1992, there should have been a greater decrease in the votes for George H. W. Bush. It is as if the popular vote for Bush collided with some type of *floor* that did not allow it to go any lower. Was there something that prevented the Republican vote from dipping lower? The answer is similar to that of the Democratic candidate's trend after 1972. There is another group of voters who essentially vote for the Republican Party's candidate, the *Republican* core or base voters.

First, an explanation of the 1992 anomaly had to be developed. The simplified explanation was similar to what occurred to the

---

[47] The linear baseline trend for the Democratic candidates could also be perceived as an upper-limit trend. This is due to the probable existence of a maximum number of voters who crossover from the Conservative electorate to vote for the Democratic candidate.

Democratic candidates after 1972, when they were stripped of most voters except for those in the core. Thus, in 1992, Republican candidate George H.W. Bush was also stripped of voters except for the Republican core.[48]

Because the 1992 election included an Independent party candidate (Ross Perot) who garnered an extraordinary number of votes, the remaining voters in the Conservative electorate were Republican core voters. These core Republican voters essentially always voted for the Republican candidate. The Independent party candidates could only have taken away a maximum number of voters from the Republican candidate before reaching the core voters. This was the reason why, despite the mirror effect, the votes for George H. W. Bush in 1992 were not lower.[49]

Second, I needed to find at least two other elections with a sizeable number of votes cast for the Independent party candidates that duplicated what occurred in 1992. These two additional elections, along with the 1992 election, could be graphed to determine if a Republican baseline trend might be revealed. Consequently, three elections were needed to reveal the Republican core baseline voting trend. Two elections would produce a line, but three is the minimum required to display a true trend.

The second election was determined quickly. It was 1968, the year that the electorate was fractured. Remember, the criterion was to find an election in which the Independent candidate obtained a substantial number of votes. In 1968, George Wallace met that criterion as a major Independent Party candidate.

The third election met the criteria as well. A review of the Independent party votes cast during the 1948 election made it stand out. In 1948, Governor James "Strom" Thurman ran for president

---

[48] As stated previously, this explanation is a simplified version of what actually took place.

[49] For further details, see *The Presidential Trend*, Chap. 6: "Defining the Baseline."

under a new third party called the States' Rights or Dixiecrat Party. (Yes, this was the same Strom Thurman who became the long-serving senator from South Carolina.) In addition, the Dixiecrats consisted mostly of individuals who splintered off from the Democratic Party because of the party's support of several controversial civil rights planks. If this sounds familiar, it should be—it was similar to the 1968 election. However, it was prior to 1968, so it was actually foreshadowing.

Thus, three elections existed that met the criteria to prove the baseline trend hypothesis. The best way to view the results was to plot these elections on a graph. Therefore, the popular vote for the Republican candidates for the elections of 1948, 1968, and 1992 were plotted (Fig. 3-1).

Once again, votes cast seemed to align themselves remarkably.[50] After I determined that all of these elections were aligned, another question arose: what if the same three elections for Democratic and Independent Party candidates were plotted on the same graph? Thus, the votes cast for the Democratic and Independent Party candidates were added to the graph. Again, the graph revealed a remarkable linear trend (see Fig. 3-2), not just for the Republican votes cast, but for the Democratic and Independent candidates' votes as well.[51]

---

[50] For further details, see *The Presidential Trend*, Chap. 9: "Analyzing the Baseline Trends."

[51] Once again, this explanation is a simplified version of what actually took place. For further details, see *The Presidential Trend*, Chap. 9: "Analyzing the Baseline Trends."

Republican Baseline Popular Vote
(1948, 1968, 1992)

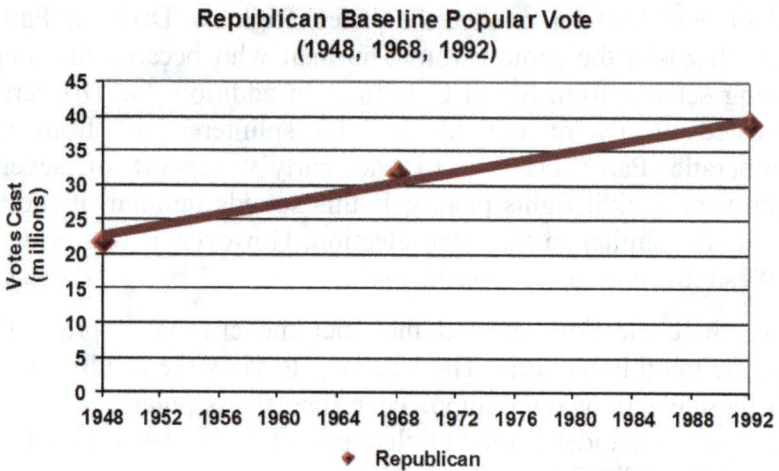

Sources: U.S. Census Bureau Statistical Abstracts 1942 to 2001 and
www.uselectionatlas.org

Figure 3-1. Republican Popular Vote (1948, 1968, 1992)

Democratic, Republican, and Independent Popular Vote
(1948, 1968, 1992)

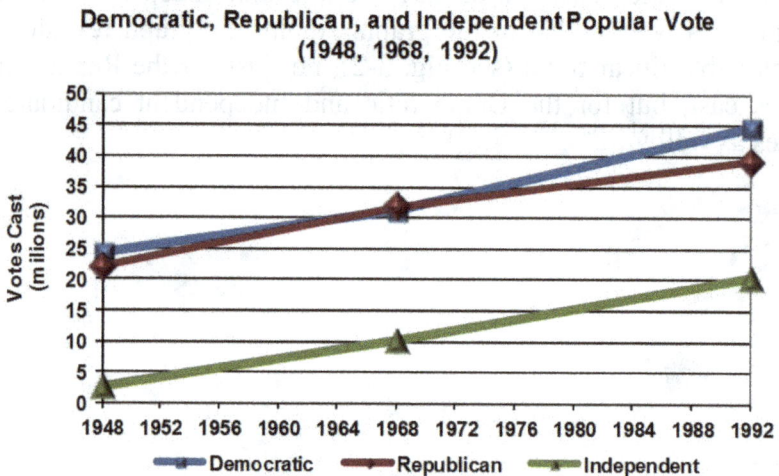

Sources: U.S. Census Bureau Statistical Abstracts 1942 to 2001 and
www.uselectionatlas.org

Figure 3-2. Democratic/Republican/Independent Popular Votes
(1948, 1968, 1992)

Although, for the most part, the trend lines were extremely linear, the Democratic and Republican baseline trends were not as linear as the Independent candidates.[52] The Democratic baseline seems to incline slightly upward, while the Republican baseline tilts slightly downward from 1968 to 1992. This upward/downward tilt was a shift in the trend line from 1968 to 1972 that gave a slightly more complex baseline.[53] Remember, the fracturing occurs in 1968 and the linear trend begins in 1972. This shift corresponds to the additional voters who voted for the Democratic candidate in 1968 but ultimately broke off in 1972.

However, regardless of the tilting, the fact that each of the political groups aligned themselves when I used the same three elections was more than a coincidence. Something had to have occurred during those three elections. What occurred was that a major Independent party candidate left only the core voters for the Democratic and Republican candidates. When these unique elections occurred, it revealed the baseline trend for these major candidates.

---

[52] The r^2 values of the Democratic, Republican, and Independent baselines are 0.98, 0.98, and 0.10, respectively.

[53] For further details, see *The Presidential Trend*, Chap. 9: "The New Democratic Baseline."

An Introduction to the Presidential Trend

Chapter 4

2016 and Future Implications

An Introduction to the Presidential Trend

Introduction

Undoubtedly, one final and probably more interesting question continues to exist and may ultimately be the most important. It is: do the effects of the trend provide any insight into future elections, including the 2016 election and beyond?

Is Demography Destiny?

Before reviewing and discussing the future implications of the presidential trend, there is an outstanding question about the past, as well as the future effect of demographics. Some say that in politics, "demography is destiny."[54] This essentially means that the demographics of a population indicate which political party will win a district, city, county, state, or even a country. Therefore, what role do demographics play in the future of the trend?

If the percentage of the popular vote is analyzed by major racial groups and plotted on a graph, the graph clearly shows several similar patterns. Using exit poll data,[55] Fig. 4-1 presents the trend lines for the percentage of each major race/ethnicity group that votes for the Progressive (or Democratic) electorates' candidates.

The trend lines versus the actual data points were used in order to identify the direction of growth or reduction. One pattern emerges readily and shows that *all* major racial/ethnicity[56] groups have trended in an *increasing* manner from 1972 to 2012 for the Progressive candidates for president (even the non-Hispanic White voting population).

---

[54] Wattenberg, B. & Scammon, R.M. 1970. *The Real Majority: An Extraordinary Examination of the American Electorate.* New York, NY: Coward McCann & Geoghegan.

[55] For further details, see *The Presidential Trend*, Chap. 14: "Did the Demographic Trends Continue after 2000?"

[56] The category of NHWhite is the population that is non-Hispanic White.

**Progressive Cand. Popular Vote Trend Lines by
Race/Ethnicity, %
(1972 to 2012 w/o 1976)**

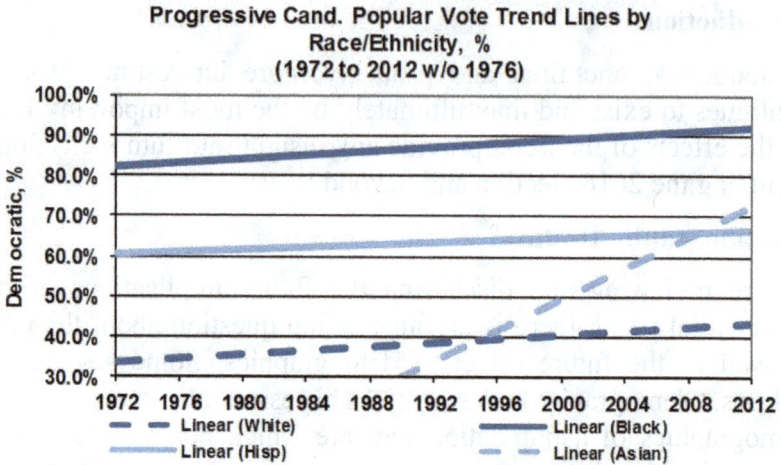

Sources: *New York Times* exit poll data (1972 to 2012) and
www.uselectionatlas.org

Figure 4-1. Progressive Cand. Popular Vote Trend Lines by
Race/Ethnicity, % (1972 to 2012, w/o 1976)

On the other hand, Fig 4-2 shows that all major racial/ethnicity groups have trended in a *decreasing* manner for the Conservative (Republican plus Independent) candidates for president. The surprising aspect of the trend lines is that from 1972 to 2012 (excluding 1976) *all major race/ethnicity groups voted in greater numbers for the Progressive electorates' candidates and lower numbers for the Conservative candidates.*

This may belie some conventional thinking today. As the Progressive candidates seem to garner more and more of the percentage of votes from all major racial groups, they also enjoy another advantage.

In addition, according to Census data, the minority population is growing at a faster rate than the general population.[57] Although all major racial/ethnicity groups are trending for the Progressive

---

[57] U.S. Census Bureau Decennial data 1970 - 2010

electorates' candidates, what can be gleamed from analyzing only the combined minority population?

Conservative Cand. Popular Vote Trend Lines by Race/Ethnicity, % (1972 to 2012 w/o 1976)

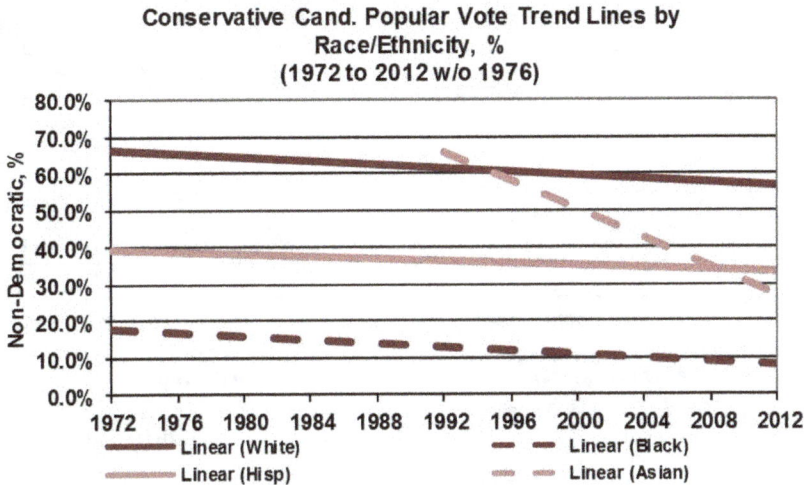

Sources: *New York Times* exit poll data (1972 to 2012) and www.uselectionatlas.org

Figure 4-2. Conservative Cand. Popular Vote Trend Lines by Race/Ethnicity, % (1972 to 2012, w/o 1976)

If the trend line for the percentage of population of minorities in the U.S. is plotted on a graph together with the Progressive (Democratic) percentage of the popular vote, once again a stark result appears (see Fig 4-3). The increase in the minority population shows an almost direct correlation with the increase in the percentage of votes cast for the Progressive candidates for president. The Conservative candidates are plotted on the same graph and show the opposite.

The graph in Fig. 4-3 shows two sets of trend lines. The dark and light blue lines represent the percentages of Progressive candidates' popular vote and minorities, respectively. The dark and light red lines represent the percentages of Conservative candidates' popular vote and non-Hispanic White (non-minorities), respectively.

Progressive/Conservative/Minority/NHWhite Trend Lines,%
(1970 to 2012 w/o 1976)

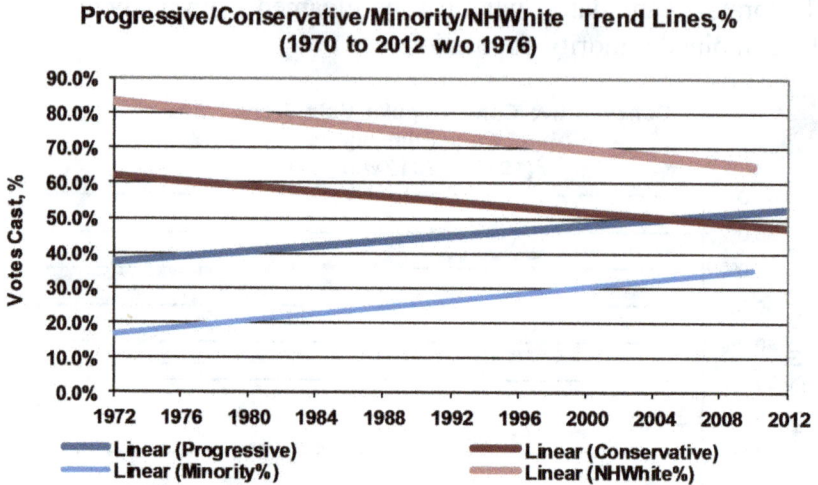

Sources: U.S. Census Bureau Decennial data 1970 - 2010 and
www.uselectionatlas.org

Figure 4-3. Progressive/Conservative/Minority/NHWhite Trend
Lines, % (1972 to 2012, w/o 1976)

When reviewing the Progressive and minority trend lines (blue), it is clear that there is an almost exact *visual* relationship between the increase in the percentage of minorities and the percentage for the Progressive candidates. Conversely, it is clear that there exists a similar relationship between the decrease in the percentage of Conservative candidates and the decrease in the percentage of non-Hispanic whites. Under normal circumstances, one could not draw any conclusions about a relationship between two parallel lines. However, when this graph is combined with the previous graph, which shows that not only is a majority of the minority vote garnered by the Progressive candidates, but a consistent *increasing* vote, the relationship is very clear.

Thus, the answer to the question of whether demography is destiny is clearly yes…*if*. Yes, because the trend lines from 1972 to 2012 show a direct correlation between the increase in the percentage of the minority population and in the percentage of the Progressive candidates' popular vote percentage. The "*if*" in the previous statement corresponds to whether or not the minority population continues to grow faster than the general population *and* if the Progressive candidates maintain their majority advantage with minority voters. If the Progressive candidates lose their majority with minority voters or better stated, if Conservative candidates gain additional minority votes, *destiny* may change. That said, even if Conservative candidates gain additional minority voters, it *might* be a moot point. As Fig. 4-1 shows, even the non-Hispanic White voters are trending for the Progressive candidates for president, albeit at a slower rate. Thus, demography may play a slightly less role than originally thought. Other factors such as policy may also be involved in the continued increase for the Progressive candidate for president.

Future Presidential Election Analysis

The final three graphs in this summary book provide a probable vision of the future and legacy of the trend. Despite the fact that the popular vote trend ended in 2000, other lingering effects continue to exist. In other words, the presidential electorate after 2000 continues to be fractured.

Before reviewing the final three graphs that reveal evidence that the fracturing remains, note that Fig 4-4 shows one of the probable reasons why these voting phenomena have gone unnoticed; the figure depicts the percentage of the popular vote for the Democratic, Republican, and Independent candidates from 1940 to 2012. When reviewing the percentage of the popular vote using the standard major three party categories (Democrat, Republican and Independent), the graph reveals no obvious trend or pattern.

However, according to the *presidential trend* theory, the analysis should also be performed using the two electorates, Progressive and Conservative, rather than the standard three. Second, the election of 1976 should be removed as an outlier or anomaly. Once these changes are made, a new graph reveals several bits of new and useful information.

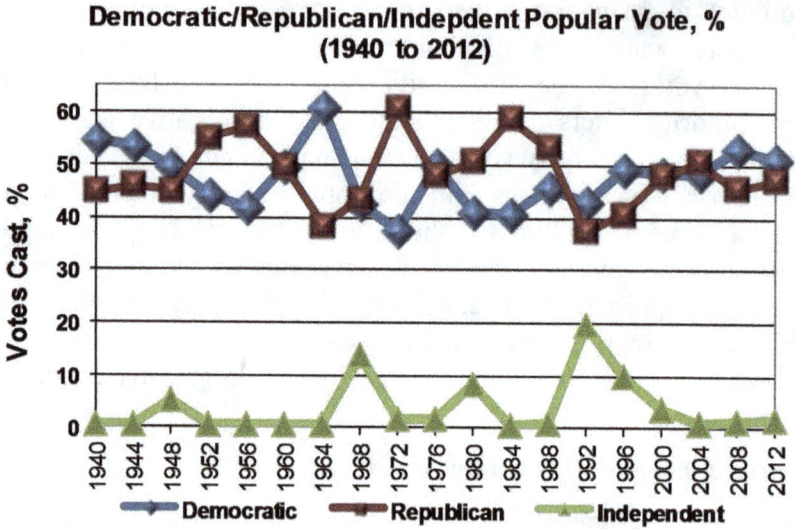

Sources: US Census Bureau Statistical Abstracts 2010 and
www.uselectionatlas.org

Figure 4-4. Democratic/Republican/Independent Candidates'
Votes Cast, % (1940 to 2012)

The new graph shows evidence of the beginning, as well as the continued fracturing, of the presidential electorate. The graph in Fig. 4-5 depicts the new paradigm of the Progressive and Conservative electorates' percentages of the popular vote. Figure 4-5 undoubtedly shows when the trend begins. From 1940 to 1968, the total Democratic and Conservative popular vote percentages fluctuate dramatically, as they should. The sinusoidal wave format corresponds to an electorate in which voters crossed back and forth between voting for the Progressive (Democrat) and Conservative (Republican and Independent) electorates. Totals for both the Progressive and the Conservative candidates rose above and fell below 50% of the vote. This provides confirmation of a *non-fractured* electorate. During this period, significant numbers of voters swung back and forth between the two different types of candidates. However, something significant occurred after 1972.

**Progressive/Conservative Electorates' Popular Vote, %
(1940 to 2012 w/o 1976)**

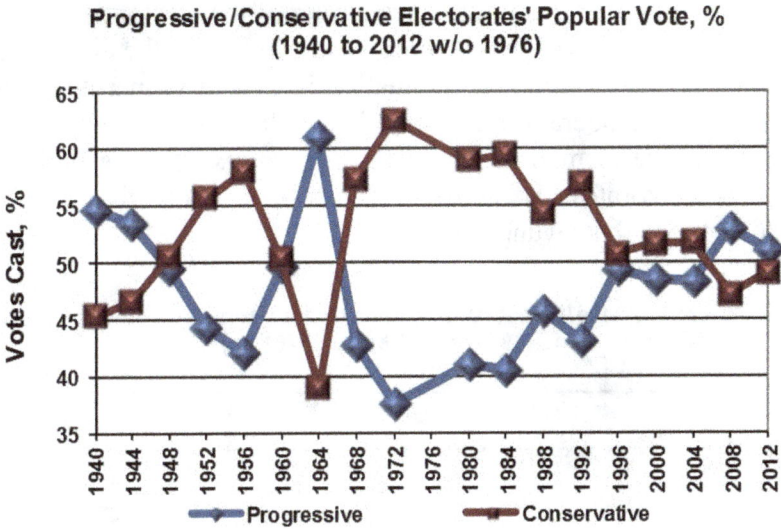

Sources: U.S. Census Bureau Statistical Abstracts 2010 and
www.uselectionatlas.org

Figure 4-5. Progressive/Conservative Electorates' Votes Cast, %
(1940 to 2012, w/o 1976)

After 1972, Fig. 4-5 shows no dramatic fluctuation of candidates' votes swinging above and below 50%. There exist only two new consistent *presidential trends* for the Progressive and Conservative popular vote percentages. One is increasing steadily while the other is decreasing. In order to view these trends more closely, examine Fig. 4-6.[58]

The new zoomed-in Fig. 4-6 shows the Progressive and Conservative electorates' percentage of votes cast from 1972 to 2012. Once again, there is no dramatic fluctuation that swings above and below 50%. Although the graph shows that the percentage of the popular vote fluctuates from election year to election year, the fluctuation is not substantial. The fluctuation is

---

[58] The 1972 to 2012 popular vote percentage trends were remarkably linear with an R-squared value of .8883.

minimized due to the continued fracturing of the electorate and the continued existence of mostly core voters in one of the electorates (Progressive). The minimal fluctuation is caused primarily by the isolation of Democratic and Republican plus Independent voters, with a relatively small number of *swing voters* crossing between the two electorates. This differs dramatically from the 1940 to 1968 elections that swung significantly.

Progressive/Conservative Electorates' Popular Vote, %
(1972 to 2012 w/o 1976)

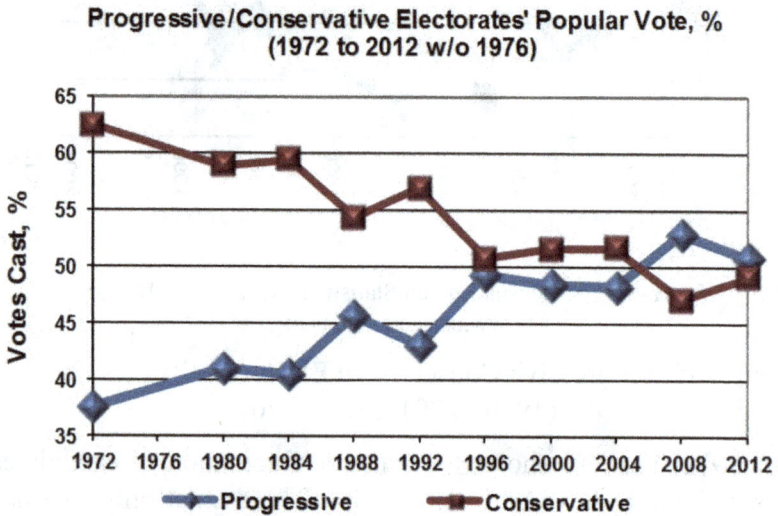

Sources: U.S. Census Bureau Statistical Abstracts 2010 and
www.uselectionatlas.org

Figure 4-6. Progressive/Conservative Electorates' Votes Cast, %
(1972 to 2012, w/o 1976)

Furthermore, the graph in Fig. 4-6 clearly displays two steady *40-year* upward and downward trends for the Progressive and Conservative electorates, respectively. In essence, the data on this startling graph show that the percentage of voters that vote for the Progressive (Democratic) candidates is increasing, while the percentage of votes for the Conservative (Republican and Independent) candidates is decreasing. In other words, the number of voters who vote for the Democratic candidates is growing faster than those who vote for the Republican and Independent candidates...*combined.*

Specifically, after the fracturing in 1972, the Progressive presidential electorate begins with much fewer voters than the Conservative electorate. However, as the total popular vote increases, the portion of voters voting for the Democratic candidates is increasing much faster than the portion that is voting for the Republican plus Independent candidates.

Finally, Fig. 4-6 may reveal another modern-day political phenomenon at the national level. Reviewing the graph, it is clear that one could have predicted many years prior the political environment in which the Progressive (Democratic) and the Conservative (for the most part Republican) popular vote would nearly equal each other. The expectation would be that major *conflict* and strife would occur during that time (as both were garnering around 50% of the vote). Could this graph explain why it appears that our national political leadership has moved to a high level of unpleasant political discourse during the past couple of decades?

In essence, to paraphrase what Sun Tzu said over two thousand years ago in the *Art of War*: *"If equally matched, do battle..."*[59] Hence, applying Sun Tzu's philosophy to the field of politics, since 1996, the current voting configuration has been primed for conflict at the congressional or presidential level (with the congressional level mimicking the conflict at the presidential). Once again, in reviewing the graph shown in Fig. 4-6, we can see that, at the national level, we have now reached a point when the Progressive and Conservative voting electorates are almost equal in size and evenly *matched*. Thus, the contentious battles at the national and congressional level could be due to this circumstance.

---

[59] Sun Tzu. 1988 *The Art of War*. Translated by Thomas Cleary. Boston, MA: Shambhula Publications

In addition, tight battles also occur at the state level. Thus, the data reinforce why some states are known as "battleground" states. Three of the primary battleground states not only show a comparable linear pattern as the national Democratic popular vote,[60] but also show similar current *percentages* of the popular vote. Florida, Ohio, and Virginia have progressed similarly to the national trends (see Fig 4-7),[61] and now have reached the point where the Progressive and Conservative electorates of the states are equally matched.

**FL, OH & VA Democratic Popular Vote, %
(1972 to 2012 w/o 1976)**

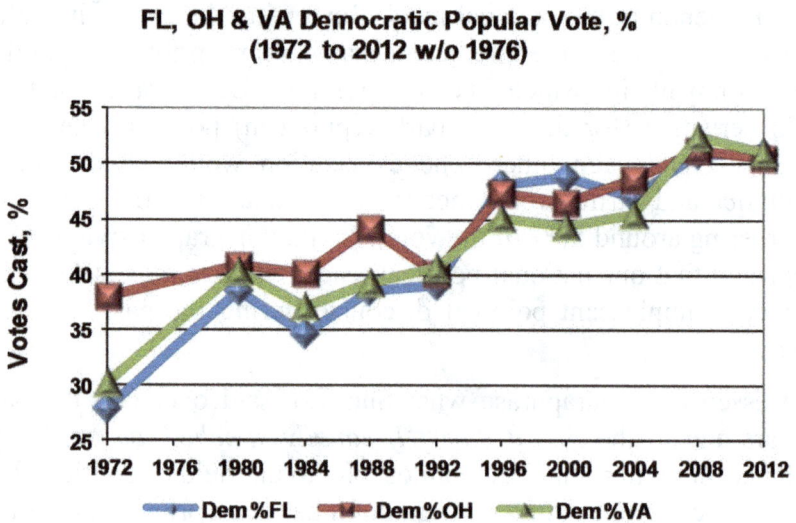

Sources: U.S. Census Bureau Current Population Surveys, 2000–2008, voting and registration in the November election, and www.uselectionatlas.org

Figure 4-7. Florida, Ohio, and Virginia Democratic Popular Vote, % (1972 to 2012, w/o 1976)

---

[60] For further details, see *The Presidential Trend*, Chap. 10: "Predictable Trend at the State Level"

[61] For further details, see *The Presidential Trend*, Chap. 15: "The Presidential Trend and Major Battleground States."

It is important to reiterate that these three states also show a linear pattern of the popular vote from 1972 to 2000 (excluding 1976).[62] If the states did not have a linear trend for the popular vote, most likely their popular vote percentage would not be significantly linear as well.

Returning to the national popular vote, barring a *major* realignment in the electorate, the national Democratic popular vote and percentage *have* or are about to consistently surpass the Republican plus Independent popular vote and percentage. Visualizing an extension of the Democratic trend in four years, or eight years, or even longer, the two will no longer be equally matched (the percentage of the Democratic popular vote should continue to exceed 50%). Clearly, the advantage will go to the Democratic candidates. Thus, after this unique point, the Democratic candidate for president should win and continue to win the popular vote until there is another significant political *realignment* in the electorate.

As a case in point, extending the trend line to predict the 2016 national popular vote percentage for the Democratic candidate projects a range between 51.9% - 56.6% (when the potential error in the trend is incorporated). Remarkably, the *40-year* trend line from 1972 to 2012 is off by only -2.6% to +2.2%.

Although not as impressive as the original presidential trend line of the popular vote, this accuracy in the percentage of the popular vote is very remarkable. Either way, the Democratic candidate appears to be poised to win the national popular vote in 2016. Nevertheless, what about the electoral vote?

Focusing on the three select battleground states yields similar results. The projected trend lines for the critical battleground states of Florida, Ohio, and Virginia yield low percentages of 52.2%, 48.5%, and 51.4%, respectively (using their trend's error

---

[62] For further details, see The Presidential Trend, Chap. 10: "Ohio and Virginia: Mini Presidential Trends."

percentages).[63] Thus, the Democratic candidate in 2016 is poised to win at least two out of the three critical battleground states.[64] The remaining percentage amounts indicate the percentage for the Conservative electorates' candidates and not the Republican candidate. The Independent candidates' percentages reduces the possible Republican candidate's projected popular vote percentage to a number lower than that for the Democratic candidate. Thus, 48.5% for Ohio may be a winning percentage for the Democratic candidate.

It is important to note that in using the trend line percentages from 1972 to 2008 to predict the 2012 election for Florida, Ohio, and Virginia yielded *low* numbers of 51.3%, 47.3%, and 49.5%, respectively. The 2012 Democratic candidate, Barack Obama, won the states with 49.9%, 50.6%, and 51.2% for Florida, Ohio, and Virginia, respectively. Two of three of the actual 2012 results were *above* the low range of the projections, with Florida the lone exception.[65]

It is also important to note that in 2012 (not 2008), Obama could have lost Florida, Ohio, and Virginia and still won the presidency. Thus, most likely, the Republican or Independent candidate must win these three battleground states (or their equivalent), plus at least one additional state in order to win the presidency.

Therefore, if the voting trends continue for these battleground states, the Democratic candidate should also win the electoral vote contest for the foreseeable future. In other words, if the U.S.

---

[63] For further details, see *The Presidential Trend*, Chap. 15: "The Presidential Trend and Major Battleground States."

[64] A GOP nomination of a person from the battleground states could certainly sway a few percentage points toward the Conservative candidate.

[65] The center trend line results as well as the high range projected values for Florida, Ohio, and Virginia exceeded the *low* range values and showed that Democratic candidates in 2008 and 2012 should win all three states. It was only when the *low* range values are used where only two of three were projected to win for the Democratic candidate.

electorate remains fractured, future Democratic candidates should enjoy success in the popular vote, electoral vote, and the U.S. presidency for many years to come.

Summary and Final Thoughts on the Trend

Although seemingly unconventional, the theory of the *presidential trend* is fairly simple and straightforward. To summarize, the polarizing issues of the turbulent sixties established the conditions whereby a significant catalyst, such as the series of civil rights laws that were passed in a relatively short time, could have theoretically splintered the country's presidential electorate into two parts.

In reality, the fracturing consisted of a group of voters (starting in 1968 and ending in 1972) shifting *away* from the Democratic presidential candidates and toward the Republican or Independent candidates or simply not voting. This monumental exodus of voters produced two theoretical electorates: the Progressive and Conservative electorates. The Progressive and Conservative electorates provided one of the new keys to analyzing voting behavior at the presidential level. Instead of analyzing elections only in terms of Democrats, Republicans, and Independents, additional insight was gleaned by dividing the analysis into *Democrats and Republicans plus Independents*.

To continue, the shift left mostly core Democratic voters voting for the Democratic candidate. This isolation of the core Democratic candidate's voters, plus steady growth in new voters and a relatively small but constant number of swing voters, led to the popular vote progressing in a *linear* manner for the Democratic candidates. The lone exception was the election of 1976, which was an outlier or anomaly.

Consequently, the *fracturing* of the electorate was actually a shift in the portion of voters away from one type of candidate, the Democratic candidate for president. In addition, the fracturing theory worked because of the existence of two core groups of voters that tended only to vote for a particular type of candidate. The Progressive electorate was isolated, with mostly core

67

Democratic voters, while the Conservative electorate contained mostly core Republican voters, in addition to a group of Independent voters.

Beside the linear nature of the Democratic popular vote, further proof of the fracturing existed in the Conservative electorate's side. Because two types of candidates were included in the Conservative electorate (Republican and Independent), rather than three, the voting pattern of the two showed a unique *mirror* effect. This distinctive mirroring existed only because there were two dominant types of candidates pulling voters away from each other. A third dominant candidate in the electorate would have significantly curtailed the mirroring effect.

It is essential to reiterate that this fracturing might not have occurred and remained in effect, if it were not for the ongoing contentious issues in the country. In other words, the original issues that existed in the sixties were not necessarily the issues that kept the presidential electorate split for 30 or even 40 years. The new *wedge issues* of the seventies, eighties, nineties, and two thousands—such as abortion, gay rights, gun control, and currently even immigration reform—most likely became supplemental, or in some cases, replacement issues for voters who kept the two electorates separated for four decades.

In addition to the new wedge issues, the original 1968 group that split off and voted for the Independent candidate, as well as their voting offspring,[66] most likely became part of the sizeable group of Independent voters in the election of 1992. Some of these voters merged into the Republican Party, but in all probability, others continued to be true *non-Democrats* and most likely exist in today's current Conservative electorate (e.g., Tea Party voters—

---

[66] Voting offspring are descendants of voters whose voting behavior is passed down from generation to generation through "family socialization."

voters who will most likely *not* vote for the Democratic candidate, but also are not core Republican voters).[67]

Finally, the path of history can sometimes be ironic. This may be the case for the presidential trend. The irony stems from the fact that the fracturing of the electorate, which was caused by a shifting away of voters, initially left the Progressive electorate with a *much* smaller number of potential voters than the Conservative electorate. However, 40 years later, the Progressive electorate is now positioned to be the larger of the two. Therefore, if the electorates continue to be fractured, the Conservative electorate will likely end up with a *much* smaller number of potential voters than the Progressive electorate. Nonetheless, regardless of the past, current, or future configuration of the electorates, the *presidential trend* remains a unique anomaly in U.S. voting history and probably the *mother of all political realignments.*

---

[67] In order to truly test the current size of the Independent Conservative voters, there needs to be another election with a major third party candidate.

An Introduction to the Presidential Trend

REFERENCES

Apple, R. W., Jr. 2004. *New York Times*. http://www.nytimes.com/2004/08/30/politics/campaign/30apple.html

Barnett, V., Lewis, T. 1994. Outliers in Statistical Data. New York, NY: John Wiley and Sons.

Bonastia, C. 2006. Knocking on the Door: The Federal Government's Attempt to Desegregate. Princeton, NJ, Princeton University Press

Breipohl, A. M. 1970. *Probabilistic Systems Analysis*. New York, NY, John Wiley & Sons

Business Week. *The Best-Known Prophet Since Daniel*. 1951. *Business Week*.

Campbell, A. 1960. *The American Voter*. Chicago, IL: University of Chicago Press.

Clymer, A. 2002. *Divisive words: News analysis; GOP'S 40 years of juggling on race*. New York Times.

Converse, P.E., Miller, W.E., Rusk, J.G. & Wolfe, A.C. 1969. *Continuity and change in American politics: Parties and issues in the 1968 election*. Wikipedia, United States Presidential Election, 1968.

Cox, Gary W. 2010. *Swing voters, core voters and distributive politics, Political Representation*, New York, NY, Cambridge University Press

Fair, R. C. 2002. *Predicting Presidential Elections and Other Things*. Palo Alto, CA: Stanford University Press.

Fairfax, T. 2013. *The Presidential Trend*. Hampton, VA: Statistical Press.

Gallup, G. & Gallup, Jr., A. 2000. The Gallup Poll 1999

Gardener, M. 2002. *Harry Truman and Civil Rights*. Carbondale, IL: Southern Illinois University Press

Gould, L. 1993. *1968: The Election that Changed America*. Chicago, IL: Ivan R. Dee, Inc.

Gravetter, F.J. & Wallnau, L.B. 1996. *Statistics for the Behavior Sciences, 4th Ed*. St. Paul, MN: West Publishing.

Greenhaven Press's Ten Book series. 2004. *The Turbulent 60s*. San Diego CA, Greenhaven Press

Hillygus D. & Shields T. 2008. *The Persuadable Voter: Wedge Issues in Presidential Campaigns*. Princeton, New Jersey: Princeton University Press.

Isserman, M. & Kazin, M. 1999. *America Divided*, New York, NY , Oxford University Press

Leip, D. 2004. *David Leip's Atlas of US Presidential Elections.* http://www.uselectionatlas.org.

Library of Congress. 2004. *African American Odyssey: The Civil Rights Era.* http://memory.loc.gov/ammem/aaohtml/exhibit/aopart9.html. Washington, D.C.

Meyers, W. P. 2004. *A Brief History of the Democratic Party.* Gualala, CA: William Peter Meyers

Moncur, M. 2005. *Michael Moncur's (Cynical) Quotations.* http://www.quotationspage.com.

Microsoft Corporation. 2005. *Vietnam War, Microsoft® Encarta® Online Encyclopedia 2005.* http://encarta.msn.com © 1997-2005.

Price, G. 2004. *Assessing the Vote and the Roots of the American Political Divide.* http://www.rationalrevolution.net/articles/assessing_the_vote_and_the_roots.htm.

Rae, N. C. 1994. *Southern Democrat.* New York, NY: Oxford University Press.

The New York Times. 2008. Edison Media Research Mitofsky International. http://elections.nytimes.com/2008/results/president/exit-polls.html.

The National Election Studies. 2000. Center for Political Studies. University of Michigan. *The NES Guide to Public Opinion and Electoral Behavior.* http://www.umich.edu/~nes/nesguide/nesguide.htm. Ann Arbor, MI: University of Michigan, Center for Political Studies [producer and distributor].

Tzu, Sun. 1988. *The Art of War.* Translated by Cleary, T. Boston, MA: Shambhula Publications.U.S. Census Bureau. 2001. *Current Population Survey.*

U.S. Census Bureau. 2002. *Demographic Trends in the 20th Century.*

U.S. Census Bureau. 2004 - 2005. *Statistical Abstract of the United States* (Table No. HS-52).

U.S. Census Bureau. 2004 - 2010. *Voting & Registration in the November 2004 Election* Online Tables.

Wattenberg, B. & Scammon, R.M. 1970. *The Real Majority: An Extraordinary Examination of the American Electorate.* New York, NY: Coward McCann & Geoghegan

INDEX